The Pentateuch

BIBLIOGRAPHIES

Craig A. Evans
General Editor

BIBLIOGRAPHIES No. 1

The Pentateuch

An Annotated Bibliography

Kenton L. Sparks

Baker Academic

A Division of Baker Book House Co
Grand Rapids, Michigan 49516

© 2002 by Kenton L. Sparks

Published by Baker Academic
a division of Baker Book House Company
P.O. Box 6287, Grand Rapids, MI 49516-6287

Printed in the United States of America

Library of Congress Cataloging-in-Publication Data
Sparks, Kenton L.
    The Pentateuch : an annotated bibliography / Kenton L. Sparks
        p.   cm. — (Bibliographies ; no. 1)
    Includes index.
    ISBN 0-8010-2398-X (pbk.)
    1. Bible. O.T. Pentateuch—Criticism, interpretation, etc.—
Bibliography. I. Title. II. IBR bibliographies ; no. 1.

Z7772.B55 S68 2002
[BS1225.52]
016.222′1—dc21   2002027722

For information about Baker Academic, visit our web site:
www.bakeracademic.com

Contents

105568

Series Preface

With the proliferation of journals and publishing houses dedicated to biblical studies, it has become impossible for even the most dedicated scholar to keep in touch with the vast materials now available for research in all the different parts of the canon. How much more difficult for the minister, rabbi, student, or interested layperson! Herein lies the importance of bibliographies and in particular this series—IBR Bibliographies.

Bibliographies help guide students to works relevant to their research interests. They cut down the time needed to locate materials, thus providing the researcher with more time to read, assimilate, and write. These benefits are especially true for the IBR Bibliographies. First, the series is conveniently laid out along the major divisions of the canon, with four volumes planned on the Old Testament, six on the New Testament, and four on methodology (see the listing of series titles on page 2). The compiler of each volume must select only the most important and helpful works for inclusion and arrange entries under various topics to allow for ease of reference. Furthermore, the entries are briefly annotated in order to inform the reader about the works' contents more specifically, once again giving guidance to the appropriate material and saving time by preventing the all too typical "wild goose chase" in the library.

Since the series is designed primarily for American and British students, the emphasis is on works written in English. Fortunately, a number of the most important foreign-language works have been translated into English, and wherever this is the case this information is included along with the original publication data. Again keeping in mind the needs of the student, we have decided to list the English translation before the original title.

These bibliographies are presented under the sponsorship of the Institute for Biblical Research (IBR), an organization of evangelical Christian scholars with specialties in both Old and New Testaments and their ancillary disciplines. The IBR has met annually since 1970; its name and constitution were adopted in 1973. Besides its annual meetings (normally held the evening and morning prior to the annual meeting of the Society of Biblical Literature), the institute publishes a journal, *Bulletin for Biblical Research,* and conducts regional study groups on various biblical themes in several areas of the United States and Canada. The Institute for Biblical Research encourages and fosters scholarly research among its members, all of whom are at a level to qualify for a university lectureship. Finally, the IBR and the series editor extend their thanks to Baker Book House for its efforts to bring this series to publication. In particular, we would like to thank David Aiken for his wise guidance in giving shape to the project.

Craig A. Evans
Acadia Divinity School

Author's Preface

For Jews and Christians alike, the Pentateuch has been—and continues to be—among the more important foci of exegetical tradition. The Torah provides Jews with foundations for covenant life, and for Christians the task of integrating this Torah with gospel has often taken center stage. While these theological issues remain important for many readers of Scripture, in modern times new questions have been asked of the text. When was the text written, and by whom? By what process was the text composed? What sources were used, and what do we know about the nature and history of those sources? What problems did the author face, and what opportunities did the author seek to exploit? How did the author (or authors) intend to arrange the text, and in what ways did the strictures of mind and language shape the text in unintended ways? What can we learn about the psychology of the author? Could the author have been a woman and, if so, how does this influence our reading of the text? Against what viewpoint was this text a polemic? How would the "original audience" have read this text, and how have differing communities subsequently read it?

There is nothing easy about choosing five hundred or so important articles and books that introduce readers to these interpretive questions and to scholarship's effort to answer them. In the case of the Pentateuch, the basic questions and problems as posed by modern scholars, as well as their supposed solutions, are often found in untranslated German monographs. Moreover, the most important English sources frequently begin, as it were, in the middle of the debate, making it difficult for uninitiated readers to appreciate the questions—much less the solutions. While I cannot pretend to solve this problem, two features in this volume may help. First, so much as is possible, each bibliographic entry offers a straightforward description of the author's basic point—if there is one—and situates this point within its scholastic milieu. Second, I have added in square brackets additional commentary and bibliography that might be of value to the reader, whether student or scholar.

What criteria were used to select these entries? First and foremost I have included "classic" works that have profoundly shaped present readings of the Pentateuch. These works are not included in a section entitled "classic works" but are instead integrated with the entries and topics to which they most directly relate. Second, I have given preference to recent works that are likely to give readers the most up-to-date picture of the debate. Third, I have attempted to provide breadth of subject matter—no small task given that the vast majority of material written on the Pentateuch covers the Book of Genesis, especially the primeval history in chapters 1–11. Finally, I have made room for works that seem to offer innovative but nonetheless promising readings of the text.

In a few cases I have elected to include important studies that do not address directly the materials in the Pentateuch itself. When I have done so, two things are always true: the study in question has important implications for the study of the Pentateuch, and I suspect that the monograph or article in question will not be addressed in another volume of the IBR Bibliography Series.

I conclude by noting that many of the most important and formative discussions in Pentateuchal research are found in commentaries, and these are not included precisely because commentaries are readily accessible and, due to their completeness, are impossible to fairly represent in brief annotations. This only serves to remind the reader: check the commentaries.

Kenton L. Sparks

Abbreviations

ABR	*Australian Biblical Review*
ACEBTSup	Amsterdamse Cahiers voor Exegese en bijbelse Theologie Supplements
AcT	*Acta theologica*
AnBib	Analecta biblica
ANET	*Ancient Near Eastern Texts Relating to the Old Testament.* Edited by J. B. Pritchard. 3d ed. Princeton, 1969
AOAT	Alter Orient und Altes Testament
AsTJ	*Asbury Theological Journal*
ATANT	Abhandlungen zur Theologie des Alten und Neuen Testaments
AUSS	*Andrews University Seminary Studies*
BA	*Biblical Archaeologist*
BAR	*Biblical Archaeology Review*
BASOR	*Bulletin of the American Schools of Oriental Research*
BBB	Bonner biblische Beiträge
BBET	Beiträge zur biblischen Exegese und Theologie
BEATAJ	Beiträge zur Erforschung des Alten Testaments und des antiken Judentum
BETL	Bibliotheca ephemeridum theologicarum lovaniensium
Bib	*Biblica*
BJS	Brown Judaic Studies
BN	*Biblische Notizen*
BRev	*Bible Review*
BSac	*Bibliotheca sacra*
BTFT	*Bijdragen: Tijdschrift voor Filosofie en Theologie*

BWANT	Beiträge zur Wissenschaft vom Alten (und Neuen) Testament
BZ	Biblische Zeitschrift
BZAW	Beihefte zur Zeitschrift für die alttestamentliche Wissenschaft
CahRB	Cahiers de la Revue biblique
CBET	Contributions to Biblical Exegesis and Theology
CBQ	Catholic Biblical Quarterly
ConBOT	Coniectanea biblica: Old Testament Series
CTQ	Concordia Theological Quarterly
EvQ	Evangelical Quarterly
FAT	Forschungen zum Alten Testament
FRLANT	Forschungen zur Religion und Literatur des Alten und Neuen Testaments
HAR	Hebrew Annual Review
HBS	Herders biblische Studien
HBT	Horizons in Biblical Theology
HSM	Harvard Semitic Monographs
HUCA	Hebrew Union College Annual
IBS	Irish Biblical Studies
IEJ	Israel Exploration Journal
Int	Interpretation
JANESCU	Journal of the Ancient Near Eastern Society of Columbia University
JAOS	Journal of the American Oriental Society
JBL	Journal of Biblical Literature
JBQ	Jewish Bible Quarterly
JCS	Journal of Cuneiform Studies
JETS	Journal of the Evangelical Theological Society
JNES	Journal of Near Eastern Studies
JNSL	Journal of Northwest Semitic Languages
JQR	Jewish Quarterly Review
JSOT	Journal for the Study of the Old Testament
JSOTSup	Journal for the Study of the Old Testament: Supplement Series
JTS	Journal of Theological Studies
KTU	Die keilalphabetischen Texte aus Ugarit. AOAT 24/1. Neukirchen-Vluyn, 1976. 2d enlarged ed. of KTU: The Cuneiform Alphabetic Texts from Ugarit, Ras Ibn Hani, and Other Places. Edited by M. Dietrich, O. Loretz, and J. Sanmartín. Münster, 1995 (= CTU)

LB	*Linguistica Biblica*
LKA	E. Ebeling and F. Köcher, *Literarische Keil-schrifttexte aus Assur* (Berlin, 1953)
MT	Masoretic Text
OBO	Orbis biblicus et orientalis
OLA	Orientalia lovaniensia analecta
OTE	*Old Testament Essays*
OtSt	Oudtestamentische Studiën
PRSt	*Perspectives in Religious Studies*
RB	*Revue biblique*
RelSRev	*Religious Studies Review*
RIDA	*Revue internationale des droits de l'antiquité*
RTP	*Revue de théologie et de philosophie*
SBL	Society of Biblical Literature
SBLDS	SBL Dissertation Series
SBLMS	SBL Monograph Series
SBLSCS	SBL Septuagint and Cognate Studies
SBLSymS	SBL Symposium Series
SBT	Studies in Biblical Theology
SJLA	Studies in Judaism in Late Antiquity
SJOT	*Scandinavian Journal of the Old Testament*
TBT	*The Bible Today*
TQ	*Theologische Quartalschrift*
TynBul	*Tyndale Bulletin*
UF	*Ugarit-Forschungen*
USQR	*Union Seminary Quarterly Review*
VT	*Vetus Testamentum*
VTSup	Vetus Testamentum Supplements
WMANT	Wissenschaftliche Monographien zum Alten und Neuen Testament
WTJ	*Westminster Theological Journal*
ZABR	*Zeitschrift für altorientalische und biblische Rechtsgeschichte*
ZAW	*Zeitschrift für die alttestamentliche Wissenschaft*

1

Texts and Versions

The most important, complete manuscripts of the Pentateuch include the Masoretic and Samaritan texts (both in Hebrew), the Greek translations (Septuagint), the Aramaic Targums, and the Latin Vulgate. Various fragmentary texts—including Hebrew texts and fragments from the Dead Sea Scrolls—are also important, as are numerous other ancient translations. The primary bibliography for these texts is provided in chapter 2 of E. C. Hostetter's volume in this series (IBR Bibliographies 11).

The entries below simply supplement those included in Hostetter. For primary publication of the Dead Sea Scrolls, see the series Discoveries in the Judean Desert (Oxford: Clarendon).

1   Ch. Heller. *The Samaritan Pentateuch.* Berlin: M. Schersow, Kirchhain, 1923.

2   B. K. Waltke. "Prolegomena to the Samaritan Pentateuch." Ph.D. diss., Harvard University, 1965; see also "Samaritan Pentateuch," *ABD* 5:932–40.

     Although the Samaritan Pentateuch has been adapted to reflect a unique viewpoint and to solve exegetical and theological problems, where the Samaritan and Greek traditions agree against the Masoretic Hebrew, the Samaritan/Greek reading should often be preferred.

3   J. D. Purvis. *The Samaritan Pentateuch and the Origin of the Samaritan Sect.* Cambridge: Harvard University Press, 1968.

     A standard discussion of the nature of the Samaritan Pentateuch. Explores the origins of the Samaritan sect and of this important text that the sect produced.

4   J. E. Sanderson. *An Exodus Scroll from Qumran: 4Qpaleo-Exod and the Samaritan Tradition.* Harvard Semitic Studies 30. Atlanta: Scholars, 1986.

Publication and detailed discussion of the Exodus manuscript, written in an archaic script, that was found at Qumran (Dead Sea Scrolls). The text is similar in many respects to the Samaritan Pentateuch.

5   A. Kamesar. *Jerome, Greek Scholarship, and the Hebrew Bible: A Study of the Quaestiones Hebraicae in Genesium.* Oxford: Clarendon, 1993.

An important discussion of Jerome, his Vulgate, and the early Christian debate over which textual tradition should take priority: Hebrew or Greek? Focus of the volume is Jerome's discussion of Genesis. [Jerome broke with church tradition by basing his Latin Vulgate on the Hebrew rather than the Greek Septuagint. Because the Vulgate is several centuries older than our oldest complete Hebrew manuscripts, this makes it an important witness to the ancient text.]

6   J. W. Wevers. *Notes on the Greek Text of Genesis.* SBLSCS 35. Atlanta: Scholars, 1993; *Notes on the Greek Text of Exodus.* SBLSCS 30. Atlanta: Scholars, 1990; *Notes on the Greek Text of Leviticus.* SBLSCS 44. Atlanta: Scholars, 1997; *Notes on the Greek Text of Numbers.* SBLSCS 46. Atlanta: Scholars, 1998; *Notes on the Greek Text of Deuteronomy.* SBLSCS 39. Atlanta: Scholars, 1995.

Five volumes that offer a detailed discussion of the Greek Pentateuch. [Wevers is perhaps the foremost authority on the Septuagint's Pentateuch.]

7   D. N. Freedman and K. A. Matthews, with contributions by R. S. Hanson. *The Paleo-Hebrew Leviticus Scroll (11Qpaleo-Lev).* Philadelphia: American Schools of Oriental Research; Winona Lake, Ind.: Eisenbrauns, 1985.

Publication and detailed discussion of fragments of Leviticus, written in an archaic script, that were found at Qumran (Dead Sea Scrolls).

2

Introductory Works

Our competence in any discipline moves from the general to the specific. The monographs, articles, and collected works in this chapter provide a general framework for appreciating modern Pentateuchal scholarship. Many topics and issues addressed in the following chapters (3–10) are addressed in these general works as well. Section 2.1 focuses on more recent works, while §2.2 emphasizes the history of the discipline.

2.1 Introductions and General Discussions

8   D. J. A. Clines. *The Theme of the Pentateuch.* JSOTSup 10. Sheffield: JSOT, 1978.

> In spite of its underlying compositeness, the final form of the Pentateuch coheres nicely as a single narrative that is thematically united. The primary theme of the Pentateuch is the partial fulfillment and, by implication, partial nonfulfillment, of the patriarchal promises and blessings. [A second edition, published in 1997, includes a reassessment by Clines.]

9   H. Wolf. *An Introduction to the Old Testament Pentateuch.* Chicago: Moody, 1991.

> Argues that the Pentateuch is very old and was written, in most of its essentials, by Moses. The volume reflects an evangelical, Christian theological viewpoint and includes a helpful summary of the history of Pentateuchal scholarship as well as a detailed discussion of the Pentateuch's content and theology.

10   J. Blenkinsopp. *The Pentateuch: An Introduction to the First Five Books of the Bible.* Anchor Bible Reference Library. New York: Doubleday, 1992.

> A good introduction by an important Pentateuchal scholar.

11   W. C. Kaiser, Jr. "Images for Today: The Torah Speaks Today." Pp. 117–32 in *Studies in Old Testament Theology.* Edited by R. L. Hubbard. Dallas: Word, 1992.

    The Pentateuch's central theme is the partial fulfillment of the patriarchal promises and the continuing expectation for complete fulfillment. [This is reminiscent of Clines's volume, *Theme of the Pentateuch,* #8].

12   A. F. Campbell and M. A. O'Brien. *Sources of the Pentateuch: Texts, Introductions, Annotations.* Minneapolis: Fortress, 1993.

    An introduction to Pentateuchal criticism along with biblical texts that have been arranged according to the standard source and redactional divisions.

13   G. L. Archer, Jr. *A Survey of Old Testament Introduction.* Updated and rev. ed. Chicago: Moody Press, 1994.

    Includes a lengthy survey of modern Pentateuchal criticism and concludes, contrary to the consensus, that Moses composed the Pentateuch in the second half of the second millennium B.C.E. [Since its appearance in 1964 (1st ed.), this volume has provided a standard evangelical response to source- and redaction-critical views of the Pentateuch's composition.]

14   J. Van Seters, *The Pentateuch: A Social-Science Commentary.* Trajectories 1. Sheffield: Sheffield Academic Press, 1999.

    A valuable introductory survey of Pentateuchal research along with a clear and simplified presentation of the author's unique approach to the Pentateuch, as expressed in his other volumes (see #51; #53; #198).

15   A. Rofé. *Introduction to the Composition of the Pentateuch.* Biblical Seminar 58. Sheffield: Sheffield Academic Press, 1999.

    A very clear and concise introduction to modern theories of Pentateuchal composition.

16   T. D. Alexander. *From Paradise to the Promised Land: An Introduction to the Pentateuch.* 2d ed. Grand Rapids: Baker; Carlisle, England: Paternoster, 2002.

    An evangelical and theologically oriented synchronic reading of the Pentateuch as a single piece of literature. Special attention is given to the theological function of the text within the Christian canon.

2.2 Surveys of Research

17   R. J. Thompson. *Moses and the Law in a Century of Criticism since Graf.* VTSup 19. Leiden: Brill, 1970.

This work surveys the scholarly discussion of Pentateuchal composition from the time of K. H. Graf until 1970. An indispensable resource for those interested in the history of Pentateuchal criticism.

18   D. A. Knight. *Rediscovering the Traditions of Israel.* Missoula, Mont.: Scholars, 1973.

Historically surveys and then critiques the traditio-historical approaches in Germany and in the Scandinavian "Uppsala circle." [Tradition history is concerned with tracing the development of a tradition from its origins to its final form in the text.]

19   J. Rogerson. *Old Testament Criticism in the Nineteenth Century: England and Germany.* London: SPCK, 1984.

An important historical survey of nineteenth-century Old Testament scholarship.

20   J. Kselman. "The Book of Genesis: A Decade of Scholarly Research." *Int* 45 (1991): 380–92.

Surveys Genesis scholarship from 1980–90.

21   E. W. Nicholson. *The Pentateuch in the Twentieth Century: The Legacy of Julius Wellhausen.* Oxford: Clarendon, 1998.

A survey of modern Pentateuchal scholarship that begins with the first critical questions raised in the eighteenth century and traces the debate until the dawn of the twenty-first century. Concludes with an assessment of contemporary scholarship and avers that the traditional view of Wellhausen (#22) remains the most convincing approach. [This survey does not include the works of Jewish scholarship and neglects readings of the text that argue for the Pentateuch's unity.]

3

Composition, Authorship, and Context

For centuries, Christian and Jewish scholars have assumed that the Pentateuch was the ancient composition of the prophet Moses. This was based on several observations. First, Moses is indicated at numerous points in the text to have written this or that down. Second, Moses is a primary character in the narrative, and Jewish tradition tended to attribute the authorship of the biblical narratives to their primary characters. Third, in the Gospels, Jesus refers to these writings as the books of Moses at numerous points. It is only in the last few centuries that scholars have raised serious questions about this traditional perspective. The first clues that a problem might exist had little to do with the author per se but with features of the text that gave it a composite look. Although some scholars have explained this as a rhetorical device used by the Pentateuch's author, this compositeness is more commonly explained by postulating that the Pentateuch was composed by various authors living in quite different historical situations. The unfolding debate about these issues and problems is covered in this section. As we will see, modern scholarship tends to view the Book of Deuteronomy as a separate composition from the rest of the Pentateuch. Consequently, the works in this section concern themselves primarily with the so-called Tetrateuch, that is, Genesis through Numbers.

3.1 General Discussions

22   J. Wellhausen, *Die Composition des Hexateuchs und der historischen Bücher des Alten Testaments.* 3d ed. Berlin:

Georg Reimer, 1899. [Although this volume does not exist in English, there are numerous translations of his closely related work, *Prolegomena zur Geschichte Israels* (Berlin: G. Reimer, 1878). See, for example, *Prolegomena to the History of Ancient Israel* (Edinburgh: A. & C. Black, 1885).] Wellhausen sets forth his classic theory of Pentateuchal composition, that the Pentateuch (indeed, the "Hexateuch" = Genesis–Joshua) was composed of four primary sources: J (ninth century B.C.E.), E (eighth century B.C.E.), D (seventh century B.C.E.), and P (fifth century B.C.E.). This allowed Wellhausen and others to use these sources to write a history of Israelite religious thought.

23 H. Gunkel. *Schöpfung und Chaos in Urzeit und Endzeit: Eine religionsgeschichtliche Untersuchung über Gen I und Ap Joh 12.* Göttingen: Vandenhoeck & Ruprecht, 1895.
A methodological critique of Wellhausen's literary approach to the Pentateuch. Stresses that our understanding of the Pentateuch and of Israelite religion cannot rest on the written literary sources but must move still further behind them in an examination of the smaller and older oral traditions that became a part of these sources. [This approach, called form criticism, sought to identify the various genres included in the Pentateuch and to identify the context (*Sitz im Leben*) within which these genres were composed and used. The goal is to reconstruct the history of traditions from their inception up to the present. For Gunkel, J and E represented schools of oral narrators who collected and recited the traditions rather than literary authors.]

24 W. H. Green. *The Higher Criticism of the Pentateuch.* New York: Scribner's, 1908.
An early evangelical analysis of, and response to, literary criticism of the Pentateuch. The features of the Pentateuch that supposedly suggest multiple authors and viewpoints are best explained on stylistic grounds. The bias of critics against the Bible's authority causes them to imagine many of the patterns that support their critical views.

25 G. von Rad. *Das formgeschichtliche Problem des Pentateuch.* BWANT 26. Stuttgart: Kohlhammer, 1938. English translation: "The Form-Critical Problem of the Hexateuch." Pp. 1–78 in *The Problem of the Hexateuch and Other Essays.* London: Oliver and Boyd, 1966.
How did the diverse materials of the Pentateuch come together into a coherent whole? Oral creeds recited at the Israelite festivals (e.g., Deut. 26:5–9) brought together the diverse elements

of Israelite tradition into brief, succinct summaries. Such a creed served as the template for the work of J, who brought together the traditions into a full-blown narrative, added the primeval history and Sinai tradition to them, and then composed his history running from Genesis to Joshua (a Hexateuch rather than a Pentateuch).

26   M. Noth. *Überlieferungsgeschichte des Pentateuch.* Stuttgart: W. Kohlhammer, 1948. English translation: *A History of Pentateuch Traditions.* Trans. B. W. Anderson. Englewood Cliffs, N.J.: Prentice-Hall, 1972.

The five basic traditional themes of the Pentateuch—the exodus, the guidance into the Land, the promises to the patriarchs, the wilderness tradition, and the Sinai theophany—originated separately and were combined at an oral level during the Judges period as they were recited in the covenant ceremonies of the ancient Israelite tribes (following the Greek model, Noth called this group of united tribes an "amphictyony"). Eventually, these traditions were written down, in the north as the work of E and in the Judean south as the work of J. These works were later combined, with J serving as the basis. In the postexilic period the Priestly writer (P) wrote his own narrative, which removed the entrance into Canaan from JE, thus allowing the conquest story of the Deuteronomistic historian (in Joshua) to provide that theme. [For a general appraisal of Noth's influence on modern scholarship, see S. L. McKenzie and M. P. Graham, eds., *The History of Israel's Tradition: The Heritage of Martin Noth,* JSOTSup 182 (Sheffield: Sheffield Academic Press, 1994).]

27   Y. Kaufmann. *The History of Israelite Religion.* 4 vols. Tel Aviv: Dvir, 1937–56 [in Hebrew]. English translation: *The Religion of Israel: From Its Beginnings to the Babylonian Exile.* Translated and abridged by Moshe Greenberg. Chicago: University of Chicago Press, 1960.

This classic discussion of Israelite religion concludes, among other things, that P is early and preexilic rather than late and postexilic. Hence, P and J are essentially contemporaries. Proposes that P did not influence preexilic Israelite literature because P was a secret Priestly document.

28   U. Cassuto. *The Documentary Hypothesis and the Composition of the Pentateuch.* Jerusalem: Magnes Press, Hebrew University, 1961. Originally published in Hebrew, 1941.

This critique of documentary theories questions the validity of the criteria used by scholars to divide the Pentateuch into various sources. Variations in the divine name, doublets, repetitions, language, and style do not suggest multiple authors or sources but are best explained as literary conventions and compositional strategies. [For a recent assessment of Cassuto's influence in the present, see A. Abela, "Umberto Cassuto's *The Documentary Hypothesis:* Thirty Years Later," *Melita Theologica* 43 (1992): 61–68.]

29 O. T. Allis. *The Five Books of Moses.* 3d ed. Philadelphia: Presbyterian and Reformed Publishing, 1964.

Argues that the rejection of Mosaic authorship of the Pentateuch has grave consequences for biblical authority. This verdict is followed by a lengthy defense of the Mosaic origins of the Pentateuch. Originally published in 1942 (2d ed., 1949).

30 F. V. Winnett. "Re-examining the Foundations." *JBL* 84 (1965): 1–19.

Questions the traditional Wellhausian view and, in a radical departure, offers a number of innovative alternatives, among them the view that J is a late rather than an early composition.

31 W. F. Albright. "Verse and Prose in Early Israelite Tradition." Pp. 1–52 in *Yahweh and the Gods of Canaan.* London: School of Oriental and African Studies, 1968. Reprint, Winona Lake, Ind.: Eisenbrauns, 1990.

The essential accuracy and historicity of the Pentateuch is guaranteed by the fact that its authors drew upon very ancient epic sources that are now lost to us.

32 H. H. Schmid. *Der sogenannte Jahwist: Beobachtungen und Fragen zur Pentateuchforschung.* Zürich: Theologischer Verlag, 1976.

The materials and traditions of the "so-called Yahwist" reflect influences from late prophetic and Deuteronomistic ideas. This suggests that the J composition is not a very old work from the Solomonic period, as von Rad thought, but a late product of the exile. [Schmid's work has exerted considerable influence on later discussions, particularly those of continental scholarship. For an English point of entry to his work, see H. H. Schmid, "In Search of New Approaches in Pentateuchal Research," *JSOT* 3 (1977): 33–42.]

33 R. Rendtorff. *Das überlieferungsgeschichtliche Problem des Pentateuch.* BZAW 147. Berlin: de Gruyter, 1977. English translation: *The Problem of the Process of Transmission in the Pentateuch.* JSOTSup 89. Sheffield: JSOT, 1990.

The basic narrative of the Pentateuch was not composed by combining parallel sources J and E, nor were there ever such lengthy sources. Instead, the various materials were joined through a tradition-historical process that began with small blocks of material and then gradually combined these into larger compositions. P represents a later redactional addition to these materials. [This approach is further elaborated in the work of E. Blum (#38; #47).]

34   D. W. Baker. "Diversity and Unity in the Literary Structure of Genesis." Pp. 197–215 in *Essays on the Patriarchal Narratives*. Edited by A. R. Millard and D. J. Wiseman. Leicester, England: InterVarsity, 1980.

Careful study of the rhetoric and structure in Genesis must precede any effort to isolate seams and fractures that might point to conflicting sources. When this is done, Genesis appears to be a carefully structured whole and, moreover, the various sections normally apportioned to sources—such as J, E, and P—presume each other at numerous points. Genesis is therefore the work of a single author.

35   M. Rose. *Deuteronomist und Jahwist.* ATANT 67. Zürich: Theologischer Verlag, 1981.

Concludes that in all cases where it is possible to determine literary dependency, J is later than, and dependent upon, both D and the Deuteronomistic History.

36   S. Tengström. *Die Toledotformal und die literarische Struktur der priesterlichen Erweiterungsschicht im Pentateuch.* ConBOT 17. Lund, 1981.

The Priestly "toledoth" formulas in the Pentateuch suggest that P should be understood as a supplemental redaction to the Pentateuch rather than as an independent narrative source.

37   A. Hurvitz. *A Linguistic Study of the Relationship between the Priestly Source and the Book of Ezekiel.* CahRB 20. Paris: Gabalda, 1982.

The linguistic features and vocabulary of P show it to be older than the early exilic prophecies of Ezekiel. Hence, contrary to conventional scholarship, P is a preexilic composition.

38   E. Blum. *Die Komposition der Vätergeschichte.* WMANT 57. Neukirchen: Neukirchener Verlag, 1984.

An exilic Deuteronomistic editor (KD = *deuteronomistiche Komposition*) created the patriarchal narratives by joining older patriarchal traditions, especially the Jacob story (which already included the Joseph story) and the Abraham story. [Considerable attention is given to the composition history of KD's sources prior to their inclusion in KD, and Blum also stresses KD's method for bringing thematic unity to these diverse sources.] KP (the *priesterliche Komposition*) represents a shorter and later alternative version of the patriarchal stories, which a later redactor combined with KD to create a kind of compromise document. [As the primary compositionist of Genesis, KD is roughly equivalent to what other scholars call J. Blum's thesis fleshes out the previous work of R. Rendtorff (see #33), but with some variation and in greater detail.]

39 J. H. Tigay. *Empirical Models for Biblical Criticism.* Philadelphia: University of Pennsylvania Press, 1985.

Source- and redaction-critical approaches to the Pentateuch are often criticized as speculative and lacking in theoretical foundations. However, empirical evidence can be adduced for the soundness of critical study of the Pentateuch.

40 Y. T. Radday and H. Shore. *Genesis: An Authorship Study.* AnBib 103. Rome: Pontifical Biblical Institute, 1985.

Statistical studies do not confirm scholarship's standard differentiation of three Tetrateuchal sources, J, E, and P. [See critical reviews in A. Abela, "The Genesis Genesis," *Melita Theologica* 39 (1988): 155–85; and G. J. Wenham, "Genesis: An Authorship Study and Current Pentateuchal Scholarship," *JSOT* 42 (1988): 3–18. Abela finds numerous difficulties with Radday/Shore, while Wenham points out that many of the observations in Radday/Shore cohere with present developments in Pentateuchal study.]

41 I. M. Kikawada and A. Quinn. *Before Abraham Was: The Unity of Genesis 1–11.* Nashville: Abingdon, 1985.

When Genesis 1–11 is compared to the Mesopotamian Atrahasis epic and examined with rhetorical criticism, the resulting picture is of an an integrated work that cannot be separated into supposed independent sources without destroying the whole. The primeval history in Genesis 1–11 is not a combination of sources P and J but is instead the composition of a single author.

42 G. Rendsburg. *The Redaction of Genesis.* Winona Lake, Ind.: Eisenbrauns, 1985.

Genesis is composed of four cycles of material that may or may not stem from a common author (primeval history, Abraham, Jacob, Joseph). Nevertheless, the arrangement of these cycles reflects a single mind and hence suggests a final unity of Genesis, reached during the early monarchy. These features are not compatible with documentary approaches to the Pentateuch. [See a critical review in A. Abela, "The Genesis Genesis," *Melita Theologica* 39 (1988): 155–85.]

43 R. N. Whybray. *The Making of the Pentateuch: A Methodological Study.* JSOTSup 53. Sheffield: Sheffield Academic Press, 1987.

The Pentateuch is the composition of a single historian working in the postexilic period. The various tensions and duplications in the Pentateuch do not point to various authors but to this historian's use of various incompatible sources.

44   T. L. Thompson. *The Origin Tradition of Ancient Israel.* Vol. 1: *The Literary Formation of Genesis and Exodus 1–23.* JSOTSup 55. Sheffield: JSOT Press, 1987.

The Pentateuch is a fictional narrative composed by combing three kinds of material into a genealogical *toledoth* structure; this narrative reached its final shape in the late seventh century. The three kinds of materials include short tales, tradition complexes (like the Jacob cycle), and longer narratives (like the Joseph story).

45   D. Damrosch. *The Narrative Covenant: Transformations of Genre in the Growth of Biblical Literature.* San Francisco: Harper & Row, 1987.

The origins of Hebrew narrative, including the Pentateuch, can be understood as an evolution from epic and chronicle to its present form. This complex tradition history is integral to the text's present meaning.

46   D. L. Christensen and M. Narucki. "The Mosaic Authorship of the Pentateuch." *JETS* 32 (1989): 465–71.

Moses was Israel's original lawgiver and the normative influence in its early history. He is therefore suitably remembered as the Pentateuch's author, even if he did not pen portions of the text.

47   E. Blum. *Studien zur Komposition des Pentateuch.* BZAW 189. Berlin: de Gruyter, 1990.

Behind the Exodus–Numbers narrative stands a combination of older traditions about the exodus and wilderness that have been brought together by an exilic Deuteronomistic editor (KD). A redactor later combined this version with the originally separate Priestly composition (KP), which provided an alternative history of early Israel. [For background, see Blum (#38). For English summary and critical response to Blum, see G. I. Davies, "The Composition of the Book of Exodus: Reflections on the Theses of Erhard Blum," in *Texts, Temples, and Traditions: A Tribute to Menahem Haran,* ed. M. V. Fox et al. (Winona Lake, Ind.: Eisenbrauns, 1996).]

48   E. Blum. "Gibt es die Endgestalt des Pentateuch?" Pp. 46–57 in *Congress Volume, Leuven, 1989.* VTSup 43. Leiden: Brill, 1991.

Synchronic readings of the Pentateuch must deal with its diachronic character, because the Pentateuch reflects no homogeneous design in its final form.

49 R. P. Gordon. "Compositeness, Conflation, and the Pentateuch." *JSOT* 51 (1991): 57–69.

Surveys various comparative texts that have been used to demonstrate that source theories of the Pentateuch's composition are valid, giving special attention to the difference between compositeness and conflation. An examination of Num. 16, which appears to be a composite text, illustrates the issues.

50 D. Garrett. *Rethinking Genesis: The Sources and Authorship of the First Book of the Pentateuch.* Grand Rapids: Baker, 1991.

Although some post-Mosaic redaction is visible in the Pentateuch, Moses was the essential author or editor of the Pentateuch and composed it using older oral and written sources.

51 J. Van Seters. *Prologue to History: The Yahwist as Historian in Genesis.* Louisville: Westminster John Knox, 1992.

J composed his basic narrative of Genesis as a work of antiquarian historiography that provided a historical prologue for Deuteronomy and the Deuteronomistic History. Features in this work point to its composition during the Babylonian exile. Hence, for Van Seters, the Pentateuchal sources developed in this order: D, J, then P.

52 J. H. Sailhammer. *The Pentateuch as Narrative: A Biblical-Theological Commentary.* Grand Rapids: Zondervan, 1992.

A detailed reading of the Pentateuch that gives special attention to its narrative structure and to the theological and literary relationships that join the various parts into a whole. The volume represents a thoroughgoing attempt to explain the diversity and complexity of the Pentateuch within the context of its traditional Mosaic authorship.

53 J. Van Seters. *The Life of Moses: The Yahwist as Historian in Exodus and Numbers.* Louisville: Westminster John Knox, 1994.

This sequel to *Prologue to History* (#51) argues that the Yahwist's narrative in Exodus–Numbers was the work of an ancient Israelite scholar living among the Babylonian exiles.

54 J. Blenkinsopp. "An Assessment of the Alleged Pre-exilic Date of the Priestly Material in the Pentateuch." *ZAW* 108 (1996): 495–518.

Surveys attempts to challenge the scholarly convention that P is postexilic. Concludes that these efforts are flawed. [For a critical response, see J. Milgrom, "The Antiquity of the Priestly Source: A Reply to Joseph Blenkinsopp," *ZAW* 111 (1999): 10–22.]

55 D. Carr. *Reading the Fractures of Genesis: Historical and*

Literary Approaches. Louisville: Westminster John Knox, 1996.

With a few variations, Carr's work follows closely the approach of E. Blum in #38 and #47. The presentation is much clearer than Blum's and less speculative, postulating a less complicated composition history for the book. Carr stresses that P was an independent narrative that was subsequently combined with the basic non-P composition (J) of Genesis. [For obvious reasons, Carr's direct influence among English readers has been much greater than that from Blum's German works.]

56   R. E. Friedman. "Some Recent Non-arguments Concerning the Documentary Hypothesis." Pp. 87–101 in *Texts, Temples, and Traditions: A Tribute to Menahem Haran.* Edited by M. V. Fox et al. Winona Lake, Ind.: Eisenbrauns, 1996.

The three most common arguments for the authorial unity of the Pentateuch falter on close examination. These flawed arguments include: (1) no other ancient documents were written in the manner envisioned in the documentary theory; (2) the rhetorical and literary structure of the whole suggests one author; (3) statistical studies suggest the Pentateuch was written by one author.

57   G. I. Davies. "The Composition of the Book of Exodus: Reflections on the Theses of Erhard Blum." Pp. 71–85 in *Texts, Temples, and Traditions: A Tribute to Menahem Haran.* Edited by M. V. Fox et al. Winona Lake, Ind.: Eisenbrauns, 1996; "K^D in Exodus: An Assessment of E. Blum's Proposal." Pp. 407–20 in *Deuteronomy and Deuteronomic Literature: Festschrift C. H. W. Brekelmans.* Edited by M. Vervenne and J. Lust. BETL 133. Louvain: Peeters, 1997.

Two recent critical evaluations of Blum's work cited in #38 and #47. Provides valuable access to Blum for non-German readers.

58   D. J. Wynn-Williams. *The State of the Pentateuch: A Comparison of the Approaches of M. Noth and E. Blum.* BZAW 249. Berlin: de Gruyter, 1997.

A very useful English introduction to the work of M. Noth and especially E. Blum (whose primary works exist only in German).

59   D. M. Carr. "Controversy and Convergence in Recent Studies of the Formation of the Pentateuch." *RelSRev* 23 (1997): 22–31.

Despite frequent claims that there is a "crisis" among scholars regarding the origins and formation of the Pentateuch, there is actually broad agreement on several basic issues. Most scholars agree that there are at least two identifiable layers of material in the Pentateuch: P and non-P. These scholars also agree that non-P (usually called J) dates well after the united monarchy and that the so-called E materials do not reflect a literary source independent of P and non-P.

60   H.-C. Schmitt. "Die Josephgeschichte und das deuterono-mistische Geschichtswerk: Genesis 38 und 48–50." Pp. 391–405 in *Deuteronomy and Deuteronomic Literature: Festschrift C. H. W. Brekelmans*. Edited by M. Vervenne and J. Lust. BETL 133. Louvain: Peeters, 1997.

Identifies a post-P, late-Deuteronomistic redaction in the Joseph story that sought to join the Pentateuch and Deuteron-omistic History into a single primary history of Israel.

61   E. T. Mullen. *Ethnic Myths and Pentateuchal Founda-tions: A New Approach to the Formation of the Penta-teuch*. SBL Semeia Studies. Atlanta: Scholars, 1997.

The Tetrateuch is a postexilic composition designed to intro-duce Deuteronomy and the Deuteronomistic History. Persian authorities encouraged its composition as a foundational ex-pression of Jewish ethnic identity. This composition drew on a variety of older sources.

62   H. Ausloos. "The Need for a 'Controlling Framework' in Determining the Relationship between Genesis–Numbers and the So-Called Deuteronomistic Literature." *JNSL* 24 (1998): 77–89.

Argues that texts which can be dated with relative accuracy—such as the Prophets—should be used as a controlling frame-work for studying the history of the Israel's major narrative tra-ditions, the Pentateuchal and Deuteronomistic History (cf. Van Seters [#64]).

63   H. C. Brichto. *The Names of God: Poetic Readings in Bib-lical Beginnings*. Oxford: Oxford University Press, 1998.

Alternations from the divine name Yahweh to Elohim in Gen-esis cannot be used to isolate discrete literary or redactional sources because there are rhetorical and ideological reasons for the variations. *Yahweh* reflects the intimate character of the deity while *Elohim* refers to the deity in his creative roles.

64   J. Van Seters. "In the Babylonian Exile with J: Between Judgment in Ezekiel and Salvation in Second Isaiah." Pp. 71–89 in *The Crisis of Israelite Religion: Transformation of Religious Tradition in Exilic and Post-exilic Times*. Edited by B. Becking and M. C. A. Korpel. OtSt 42. Leiden: Brill, 1999.

The materials in Ezekiel and Deutero-Isaiah provide a controlling

historical and ideological framework for dating J. Ezekiel did not
know J at the exile's beginning, and at the exile's end Deutero-Isaiah did know J. Hence, J should be dated during the exile.

65 K. Schmid. *Erzväter und Exodus: Untersuchungen zur
doppelten Begründung der Ursprünge Israels innerhalb
der Geschichtsbücher des Alten Testaments.* WMANT 81.
Neukirchen-Vluyn: Neukirchener Verlag, 1999.

The "primary history" (Genesis to 2 Kings) is the compositional work of a post-P redactor during the Persian period. This
redactor took up P's independent narrative of early Israel's history and combined it with other blocks of material, including
the primeval history, the patriarchal stories, the exodus/wilder-
ness/conquest tradition, and the Books of Judges and Samuel/
Kings. [This approach is increasingly influential, especially in
continental scholarship.]

66 G. J. Wenham. "The Priority of P." *VT* 48 (1999): 240–58.

Contrary to the more common view, a careful examination of
Genesis reveals that J is supplemental to the older P narrative.
Hence, P should be dated before J.

67 T. L. Thompson. "Historiography in the Pentateuch."
SJOT 13 (1999): 253–83.

The genre of the Pentateuch is mythological speculation rather
than historiographic composition. Its primary concern is to explore the relationship between two polarities introduced in
Gen. 1:2: what is real (God's creative spirit) and what is not real
(the formlessness prior to creation).

68 T. Römer and M. Z. Brettler. "Deuteronomy 34 and the
Case for a Persian Hexateuch." *JBL* 119 (2000): 401–19.

The final chapter of Deuteronomy reflects three different authors: (1) the Deuteronomistic Historian as he provides a transition from Moses to Joshua (vv. 1*, 4*, 5–6); (2) Persian-period
efforts to create a Hexateuch (vv. 1*, 7–9); (3) the final redaction
of the Pentateuch, which conceptually rejected the Hexateuch
and therefore effected a division between Deuteronomy and
Joshua by ending the Pentateuch with Moses' death (vv. 1–3*,
4*, 10–12).

69 D. N. Freedman, J. C. Geoghegan, and M. M. Holman. *The
Nine Commandments: Uncovering a Hidden Pattern of
Crime and Punishment in the Hebrew Bible.* New York:
Doubleday, 2000.

A single editor was responsible for the final form of the primary
history (Genesis–2 Kings). According to this editor, Israel's violation of all ten commandments (i.e., "coveting") resulted in
the punishment of the exile.

70 A. Nahkola. *Double Narratives in the Old Testament: The Foundations of Method in Biblical Criticism.* BZAW 290. Berlin and New York: de Gruyter, 2001.

Since the dawn of modern biblical criticism, duplicate stories have been used to identify sources in the Pentateuch. Some scholars have resisted this trend, attributing the doublets to literary artistry or compositional technique. Neither approach is entirely correct, for there appear to be various reasons for the presence of "doublets" in the text.

3.2 Individual Components of the Pentateuch

Selections in this section supplement those referred to in 3.1 by providing more detailed discussions of the major sources that are supposedly nested in the Pentateuch.

3.2.1 The Yahwist

71 R. Rendtorff. "The 'Yahwist' as Theologian? The Dilemma of Pentateuchal Criticism." *JSOT* 3 (1977): 2–9.

Critiques von Rad's thesis that a single Yahwist compiled the basic narrative Pentateuch. The major blocks of tradition (e.g., patriarchs, exodus) reflect very different concerns and priorities, not a single viewpoint, as von Rad would have us believe. This article provides a useful introduction to the views of Rendtorff, which are more fully presented in #33.

72 R. B. Coote and D. R. Ord. *The Bible's First Historian.* Philadelphia: Fortress, 1989.

The Yahwist's narrative was a historical "apologia" for David's new kingdom, centered in Judah.

73 J. Van Seters. "The Theology of the Yahwist: A Preliminary Sketch." Pp. 219–28 in *"Wer ist wie du, Herr, unter den Göttern?" Studien zur Theologie und Religionsgeschichte für Otto Kaiser zum 70. Geburtstag.* Edited by I. Kottsieper et al. Göttingen: Vandenhoeck & Ruprecht, 1994.

J's work drew on the classical prophetic tradition and on the earlier works of Deuteronomy and the Deuteronomistic History in order to compose an early history of humanity and Israel with a more universalistic perspective. J's exilic composition influenced the thought of Second Isaiah.

3.2.2 The Elohist

In recent years, the very existence of an E source has been questioned by most scholars. E is more commonly viewed as

source material used by J. The entries below include those arguing for the existence of a discrete E source.

74   M. Lichtenstein. "Dream-Theophany and the E Docu-
         ment." *JANESCU* 1 (1969): 45–54.
         A careful reading of the Pentateuch and comparative Near East-
         ern texts suggests that "dream theophany" does not provide a
         valid criterion for distinguishing a so-called E document.

75   A. W. Jenks. *The Elohist and North Israelite Traditions.*
         SBLMS 22. Missoula, Mont.: Scholars, 1977.
         Provides evidence for a close connection between E and other
         North Israelite traditions. [This thesis supports the older view
         that E was an independent narrative source composed in the
         northern kingdom.]

76   S. E. McEvenue. "The Elohist at Work." *ZAW* 96 (1984):
         315–32.
         On the basis of style, structure, and viewpoint, the three stories
         in Gen. 20–22 (wife-sister story, Hagar's expulsion, sacrifice of
         Isaac) can be attributed to a common author, E. E's work as-
         sumed that of J and hence is best viewed as a redactional addi-
         tion that sought to emphasize God's love within the earlier
         Abraham story of J.

77   R. K. Gnuse. "Dreams in the Night—Scholarly Mirage or
         Theophanic Formula?: The Dream Report as a Motif of the
         So-Called Elohist." *BZ* 39 (1995): 28–53.
         A series of Elohistic dream reports and associated references to
         them reflect a uniform pattern consistent with the idea of an E
         source in the Pentateuch.

78   R. K. Gnuse. "Redefining the Elohist?" *JBL* 119 (2000):
         201–20.
         Responds to the growing consensus that E does not exist. Ar-
         gues that E is not only a discernible document but that it can
         also be associated with a clear context: northern prophets
         working in the seventh century B.C.E. after the fall of Israel.

3.2.3 The Priestly Writer

There is broad agreement among Pentateuchal scholars that
P exists and that it can be theologically and textually distinguished from "non-P." The primary point of debate is whether P
originated as an independent narrative that was subsequently
combined with non-P, or as a redactional stratum added to non-
P. Another locus of debate is whether P is late and postexilic (so
most scholars) or early and preexilic (a few scholars).

79 E. Auerbach. "Die babylonische Datierung im Pentateuch und das Alter des Priester-Kodex." *VT* 2 (1952): 334–42.

The Babylonian dating system (number of month + number of day) first appears in Judah around 605 B.C.E. Because P uses this system, P must date after 605.

80 Ch. Cohen. "Was the P Document Secret?" *JANESCU* 1 (1969): 39–44.

A comparison of P with an Akkadian ritual prescription suggests that they are of the same genre and that, moreover, the colophon of the Akkadian texts claims that it was a "secret" document. Hence, Y. Kaufmann's thesis (#27) that P was an early but secret document seems reasonable.

81 S. E. McEvenue. *The Narrative Style of the Priestly Writer.* AnBib 50. Rome: Biblical Institute Press, 1971.

A detailed study of P's character, style, and arrangement. Concludes that P often depends on and closely follows the work of J, but in other cases it deviates from J markedly. P's use of repetitive and formulaic language is reminiscent of fairy tales.

82 F. M. Cross. "The Priestly Work." Pp. 293–325 in *Canaanite Myth and Hebrew Epic.* Cambridge: Harvard University Press, 1973.

P was a supplementer and redactor of JE and never existed as an independent document. Similarities between P and Ezek. 40–48 suggest that P was composed during the late exile. [For a response, see E. W. Nicholson, "P as an Originally Independent Source in the Pentateuch," *Irish Biblical Studies* 10 (1988): 192–206.]

83 A. Hurvitz. "The Evidence of Language in Dating the Priestly Code." *RB* 81 (1974): 24–56.

Although P is usually dated to the postexilic period, a selective study of P's language demonstrates that P is probably preexilic, for it neither reflects nor anticipates exilic and postexilic contexts.

84 J. Blenkinsopp. "The Structure of P." *CBQ* 38 (1976): 275–92.

A detailed discussion of P's organization that suggests P should be viewed as a source rather than as a redactional layer of the Pentateuch.

85 G. Rendsburg. "Late Biblical Hebrew and the Date of 'P.'" *JANESCU* 12 (1980): 65–80.

Contrary to the thesis of Polzin, which considers P's language late, P is written in "classical biblical Hebrew" that is similar to that in the supposedly older sources J and E. [See R. Polzin, *Late Biblical Hebrew: Towards an Historical Typology of Biblical Hebrew Prose*, HSM 12 (Missoula, Mont.: Scholars, 1976).]

86   J. A. Emerton. "The Priestly Writer in Genesis." *JTS* 39
           (1988): 381–400.
           P originated as an independent document rather than as a
           redactional addition to the earlier J narrative.

87   R. B. Coote and D. R. Ord. *In the Beginning: Creation and
           the Priestly History.* Minneapolis: Fortress, 1991.
           This introduction to the Priestly writer assumes that P is a sup-
           plement to the J and E sources that originated among Zadokite
           priests in the postexilic period. Includes a close reading of P's
           theological themes (e.g., creation, Sabbath, blood, circumci-
           sion, tabernacle) and their relationships to each other.

88   F. H. Gorman, Jr. *The Ideology of Ritual: Space, Time, and
           Status in Priestly Theology.* JSOTSup 91. Sheffield: JSOT,
           1990.
           The primary role of Priestly ritual was to maintain order and re-
           store equilibrium to the ritual status of Israel.

89   S. A. Geller. "Blood Cult: Toward a Literary Theology of
           the Priestly Work of the Pentateuch." *Prooftexts* 12 (1992):
           97–124.
           In P's view, humanity marred God's original creation. Blood is
           the cleansing agent for atonement in P. P's allowance for killing
           animals after the flood was a temporary provision until the sac-
           rificial system could be implemented at Sinai. Atonement is
           available through both the regular sacrifices and the "re-cre-
           ation" via *yom kippur* (Day of Atonement).

90   A. F. Campbell. "The Priestly Text: Redaction or Source."
           Pp. 32–47 in *Biblische Theologie und gesellschaftlicher
           Wandel: Für Norbert Lohfink, SJ.* Edited by G. Braulik.
           Freiburg: Herder, 1993.
           Critiques three major proponents of the theory that P is a redac-
           tional layer of the Pentateuch rather than a source (F. M. Cross,
           R. Rendtorff, and E. Blum). Concludes against them that the
           data "do not offer encouragement to those who see P as a redac-
           tional layer" (45).

91   P. P. Jenson. *Graded Holiness: Key to the Priestly Concep-
           tion of the World.* JSOTSup 106. Sheffield: JSOT, 1992.
           The "holiness spectrum" of P is a continuum that moves from
           very holy, to holy, to clean, to unclean, to very unclean.

4

Genesis

In much of early Jewish and Christian tradition, Genesis was read as a historically accurate depiction of early human and Israelite history. Although this remains the case among some scholars, studies of the composition, authorship, and date of the Pentateuch have altered this traditional consensus. At this point, serious questions have been raised concerning the historicity of nearly every major tradition in the Pentateuch, including the stories of the primeval history in Gen. 1–11 (creation, fall, flood, Babel), the patriarchal narratives, the exodus, and the traditions about Sinai. While some scholars view this as a negative or even harmful outcome, this historical pessimism has led to an enhanced appreciation of the Pentateuch's literary and theological dimensions. The following articles and monographs outline this discussion as it pertains to Genesis.

4.1 General Discussions

92   R. L. Cohn. "Narrative Structure and Canonical Perspective in Genesis." *JSOT* 25 (1983): 3–16.

In Genesis, the divine-human relationship evolves from the never-never land of Eden, where God is tangibly present, to the world of exile, where Joseph and his brothers unwittingly serve as agents of divine providence.

93   Z. Jagendorf. "'In the Morning, Behold, It Was Leah': Genesis and the Reversal of Sexual Knowledge." *Prooftexts* (1984): 187–92.

In the episodes of Lot and his daughters (Gen. 19), Jacob's wedding night (Gen. 29), and Judah and Tamar (Gen. 38), men are duped into sexual relations with women. This motif plays on the reversal of sexual knowledge in the paradise story of Gen. 3. In the case of Jacob, the deception by which he had relations with Leah is narrative payback for his deception of Isaac in Gen. 27.

94   J. P. Fokkelman. *Narrative Art in Genesis: Specimens of Stylistic and Structural Analysis*. 2d ed. Sheffield: JSOT, 1991. Original edition: Assen: Van Gorcum, 1975.
Structuralist readings of the Book of Genesis.

95   N. C. Hable and S. Wurst, eds. *The Earth Story in Genesis*. Earth Bible 2. Sheffield: Sheffield Academic Press, 2000.
A collection of environmentally conscious readings of Genesis.

4.2 Composition, Authorship, and Context

These entries supplement those found in chapter 3.

96   T. D. Alexander. *Abraham in the Negev: A Source-Critical Investigation of Genesis 20:1–22:19*. Carlisle, England: Paternoster, 1997.
A careful reading and evaluation of Gen. 20:1–22:19 calls into question documentary theories of the Pentateuch's origins.

97   G. A. Rendsburg. "Reading David in Genesis." *BRev* 17, no. 1 (2001): 20–33
Genesis was written to address theological and political issues associated with the rise of David and Solomon. The Hebrew of Genesis is consistent with this tenth-century B.C.E. date.

4.3 The Primeval History: Genesis 1–11

In the primeval history we have a generic potpourri that includes myths, legends, genealogies, chronologies, and various etiologies; moreover, as the name "primeval history" implies, Gen. 1–11 is often viewed as a historiographic composition. Interpretive conundrums also abound in this portion of Genesis, which nevertheless plays a foundational role in many theological systems.

4.3.1 Ancient Near Eastern Myth and the Primeval History

The biblical stories of creation, fall, flood, and Babel are commonly believed to reflect influences from Near Eastern myth and legend. Most of the scholarly interest has been focused on the Gilgamesh epic, Atrahasis, *Enuma Elish*, and Adapa, but there are also many other relevant Near Eastern texts. The tendency at present is to view the biblical myths as polemics against Near Eastern myth, but there are many exceptions to this viewpoint.

98 B. S. Childs. *Myth and Reality in the Old Testament.* Naperville, Ill.: Alec R. Allenson, 1960.
Genesis (and the Old Testament) demythologized older Near Eastern traditions because Israel's view of reality was opposed to the mythical.

99 W. G. Lambert. "The Babylonian Background of Genesis." *JTS* 16 (1965): 287–300.
A comparison of Genesis with Near Eastern myths reflects both similarities and differences, but Genesis shows no knowledge of Mesopotamian traditions dating earlier than 1500 B.C.E.

100 S. N. Kramer. "The 'Babel of Tongues': A Sumerian Version." *JAOS* 88 (1968): 108–11.
In Sumerian tradition, as in Genesis, human languages are the consequence of divine intervention. [For a later and more complete translation of the text, see pages 275–319 in Th. Jacobsen, *The Harps That Once . . .* (New Haven: Yale, 1987).]

101 G. F. Hasel. "The Significance of the Cosmology in Genesis I in Relation to Ancient Near Eastern Parallels." *AUSS* 10 (1972): 1–20.
Gen. 1 employs terms and motifs from the Near Eastern mythic tradition but fills them with new meaning in an antimythical polemic.

102 J. W. Roberson. *Myth in Old Testament Interpretation.* BZAW 134. Berlin and New York: de Gruyter, 1974.
Surveys the nineteenth- and twentieth-century process by which myth became an important generic concept in OT interpretation. Includes discussions of comparative mythology, H. Gunkel, the so-called Myth-Ritual School, structuralism, and Ricoeur's symbolic interpretation of myth, among others.

103 D. P. Scaer. "The Problems of Inerrancy and Historicity in Connection with Genesis 1–3." *CTQ* 41 (1977): 21–25.
In contrast to common tendencies among scholars, argues that Gen. 1–3 must be read as history.

104 T. Frymer-Kensky. "What the Babylonian Flood Stories Can and Cannot Teach Us about the Genesis Flood." *BAR* 4, no. 4 (1978): 32–41.
The basic structures of the Atrahasis Epic and Gen. 1–9 are very similar, with both following the pattern of creation—problem—flood—solution. The flood story of Atrahasis is more similar to the Genesis flood than either the Sumerian or Gilgamesh flood tales.

✓ **105** I. Rapaport. *Tablet XI of the Gilgamesh Epic and the Biblical Flood Story: A Refutation of the Generally Held View That Genesis Chapters 6–9 Is Based upon a Babylonian Prototype.* Tel Aviv: Tel Aviv University, 1981.

The biblical flood story is commonly believed to depend on the flood story in the Gilgamesh epic. However, the two stories are different at points and, where they are very similar, this is because the biblical tradition influenced the Gilgamesh epic.

106 N.-E. Andreasen. "Adam and Adapa: Two Anthropological Characters." *AUSS* 19 (1981): 179–94.

Similarities between Adam and Adapa suggest that their stories might stem from common origins, but in their present form the two traditions present very different views of humanity.

107 R. A. Oden, Jr. "Divine Aspirations in Atrahasis and in Genesis 1–11." *ZAW* 93 (1981): 197–216.

Atrahasis was chiefly concerned with the development of the distinction between humanity and divinity. Human attempts to contravene this distinction resulted in a divine response to quell the problem. In these respects, Atrahasis and Gen. 1–11 share numerous motifs.

108 J. O'Brien and W. Major. *In the Beginning: Creation Myths from Ancient Mesopotamia, Israel, and Greece.* Chico, Calif.: Scholars Press, 1982.

An important description and comparison of various ancient and Near Eastern creation traditions.

109 P. D. Miller. "Eridu, Dunnu, and Babel: A Study in Comparative Mythology." *HAR* 9 (1985): 227–51.

A comparative study of several Mesopotamian myths and the materials found in the Primeval History of Gen. 1–11. Special attention is given to the "Eridu Genesis" (= Sumerian flood story) and the "Harab Myth." Concludes that Genesis is similar to Near Eastern primeval traditions but also differs from them at points.

110 A. Draffkorn Kilmer. "The Mesopotamian Counterparts of the Biblical Nĕpīlîm." Pp. 39–43 in *Perspectives on Language and Text: Essays and Poems in Honor of F. I. Andersen's Sixtieth Birthday.* Edited by E. W. Conrad and E. G. Newing. Winona Lake, Ind.: Eisenbrauns, 1987.

The Mesopotamian antediluvian sages, the semi-divine *apkallu*, represent the counterpart of the biblical *nephalim* in Gen. 6:1–4.

111 U. Rüterswörden. "Der Bogen in Genesis 9: Militärhistorische und traditionsgeschichtliche Erwängungen zu einem biblischen Symbol." *UF* 20 (1988): 247–63.

> Surveys various views of the "bow" imagery in Gen. 9 and concludes, with the old view of Wellhausen, that the bow (which represents divine power in ancient Near Eastern mythology) represents the unstrung, composite weapon of God that God would never again wield against creation. This suits P's more general antipathy for military violence.

112 J. C. de Moor. "East of Eden." *ZAW* 100 (1988): 105–11.

> Two Ugaritic texts, *KTU* 1.100 and 1.107, suggest that a paradise myth similar to that in Gen. 2–3 was known at Ugarit (second millennium B.C.E.).

113 J. D. Currid. "An Examination of the Egyptian Background of the Genesis Cosmogony." *BZ* 35 (1991): 18–40.

> Like Gen. 1, Egyptian creation stories, particularly the Memphite Theology, reflect a single creator deity, creation through the deity's spoken word, and creation through separation of heaven and earth. In this respect, Egyptian myths provide the closest exemplars to the creation story of Gen. 1.

114 S. W. Holloway. "What Ship Goes There: The Flood Narrative in the Gilgamesh Epic and Genesis Considered in Light of Ancient Near Eastern Temple Ideology." *ZAW* 103 (1991): 328–55.

> The ark in the Gilgamesh epic is modeled after the structure of Mesopotamian ziggurat temples, while the Genesis ark reflects the structure of Solomon's temple.

115 B. F. Batto. *Slaying the Dragon: Mythmaking in the Biblical Tradition.* Louisville: Westminster John Knox, 1992, 1–101.

> J's primeval history (Gen. 1–11) consciously borrowed and adapted motifs from both the Atrahasis and Gilgamesh epics. P's revision of J's story then drew elements from the Mesopotamian creation myth, *Enuma Elish.*

116 A. S. Kapelrud. "You Shall Surely Not Die." Pp. 50–61 in *History and Tradition of Early Israel: Studies Presented to Eduard Nielsen.* Edited by A. Lemaire and B. Otzen. VTSup 50. Leiden: Brill, 1993.

> A comparative study of the creation/fall in Gen. 2–3 and two Near Eastern stories, Adapa and Gilgamesh.

117 B. F. Batto. "The Institution of Marriage in Genesis 2 and in *Atrahasis*." *CBQ* 62 (2000): 621–31.

> Gen. 2 reflects a concern for the institution of marriage that is similar to and probably adopted from Atrahasis. However,

Genesis is more concerned with the relational aspect of marriage while Atrahasis was focused on its procreative character.

4.3.2 Genealogies in the Primeval History

Although the biblical genealogies were for many centuries viewed as historically accurate depictions of primal humanity and early Israel, the modern anthropological study of genealogies has rendered this view obsolete. There is now broad agreement that genealogies are shaped by sociological and ideological forces, as well as by the inevitable fluidities in oral, and to some extent written, traditions. The standard discussion of biblical genealogies is still R. R. Wilson, *Genealogy and History in the Biblical World* (New Haven: Yale, 1977).

118 W. H. Green. "Primeval Chronology." *BSac* 47 (1890): 285–303.

Genesis does not provide complete chronological data prior to the time of Abraham, nor can the precise date of the flood or creation be ascertained from it.

119 J. Simons. "The 'Table of Nations' (Gen 10): Its General Structure and Meaning." Pp. 155–84 in *Oudtestamentische Studiën.* Edited by P. A. H. de Boer. OtSt 10. Leiden: Brill, 1954.

The original core of the Table of Nations can be identified by its genealogical citation formula, the Hebrew *bene* plus a personal name, and it includes the families of Japheth, Ham, and Shem. The rationale behind the arrangement is geographical. This enumeration of the original Table of Nations corresponds closely to that usually apportioned to the J document of the Pentateuch.

120 M. Barnouin. "Recherches numériques sur la généalogie de Gen. V." *RB* 77 (1970): 347–65.

The unusually long life spans of the antediluvian patriarchs were derived from Babylonian astronomical data, namely, from the synodic periods of planets.

121 A. Malamat. "Tribal Societies: Biblical Genealogies and African Lineage Systems." *Archives européennes de sociologie* 14 (1973): 126–36.

The segmented genealogies of Genesis are comparable to the oral genealogies used in African tradition.

122 G. F. Hasel. "The Genealogies of Gen 5 and 11 and Their Alleged Babylonian Background." *AUSS* 16 (1978): 361–74.

The genealogies of Gen. 5 and 11 are only superficially similar to Mesopotamian texts, such as the Sumerian King List.

123 J. M. Sasson. "A Genealogical 'Convention' in Biblical Chronology?" *ZAW* 90 (1978): 171–85.

Hebrew genealogies were often constructed so that important individuals occupied the seventh or, to a lesser extent, the fifth position.

124 J. Walton. "The Antediluvian Section of the Sumerian King List and Genesis 5." *BA* 44 (1981): 207–8.

When the chronological material in Gen. 5 is converted to the Sumerian sexagesimal number system, it yields a total of 241,200 years, the same as the comparable portion of the Sumerian King List. It is therefore possible that the list of primeval kings in the Sumerian King List and the list of primeval patriarchs in Gen. 5 were both derived from a common list.

125 B. Goodnick. "Parallel Lists of Prediluvian Patriarchs." *Dor le Dor* 13 (1984): 47–51.

Although the genealogies in Gen. 4 and 5 may appear to be variants of the same tradition, the two genealogies represent their corresponding personalities quite differently: the progeny of Cain are "sons of men" while the progeny of Kenan are "sons of God."

126 B. Oded. "The Table of Nations (Genesis 10)—A Socio-cultural Approach." *ZAW* 98 (1986): 14–31.

A common older tradition lies behind the J and P versions of the so-called Table of Nations in Gen. 10. The original genealogy reflected a threefold division, including Shem (father of the sons of Heber), Ham (father of urban populations and imperial kingdoms), and Japheth (father of Gentile peoples). This threefold division was derived from Gen. 4:20–22, which originally envisioned humanity as three distinct professional classes.

127 D. T. Bryan. "A Reevaluation of Gen 4 and Gen 5 in the Light of Recent Studies in Genealogical Fluidity." *ZAW* 99 (1987): 180–88.

The genealogies in Gen. 4 and 5 are often viewed as variants of a common original. Their similarities stem instead from the partial conflation of two originally separate genealogies.

128 D. L. Christensen. "Biblical Genealogies and Eschatological Speculation." *PRSt* 14 (1987): 59–65.

The chronological system of Genesis is "not to be taken as mere historical memory. The mysterious numbers are theological statements that contain within them a look into the future as well as the distant past" (65).

129 R. S. Hess. "The Genealogies of Genesis 1–11 and Comparative Literature." *Bib* 70 (1989): 241–54.

Biblical genealogies differ in important ways from both the Mesopotamian kings list and the genealogies of the Pseudo-Hesiodic *Catalogue of Women*. In light of this, studies should focus more on comparisons of the biblical names with the onomastic evidence from the Near East.

130 C. J. Labuschagne. "The Life Spans of the Patriarchs." Pp. 121–27 in *New Avenues in the Study of the Old Testament: A Collection of Old Testament Studies, Published on the Occasion of the Fiftieth Anniversary of the Oudtestamentisch Werkgezelschap and the Retirement of Prof. Dr. M. J. Mulder*. Edited by A. S. van der Woude. OtSt 25. Leiden and New York: Brill, 1989.

The antediluvian patriarchal ages in the primeval history were derived from either Babylonian astronomical data or from a formula that added 840 (120×7; cf. Gen. 6:3) to the normal ages of those listed. The ages of the patriarchs from Abraham to Joseph are also explained formulaically: Abraham ($175 = 7 \times 5^2$), Isaac ($180 = 5 \times 6^2$), Jacob ($147 = 3 \times 7^2$), Joseph ($110 = 1 \times 5^2 + 6^2 + 7^2$).

131 T. D. Alexander. "From Adam to Judah: The Significance of the Family Tree in Genesis." *EvQ* 61 (1989): 5–19.

In its final form, the genealogical structure of Genesis is focused on the ancestry of David's royal house.

132 W. Horowitz. "The Isles of the Nations: Genesis X and Babylonian Geography." Pp. 35–43 in *Studies in the Pentateuch*. Edited by J. A. Emerton. VTSup 41. Leiden: E. J. Brill, 1990.

Several distant nations in the genealogy of Japheth (Gen. 10:2–4) appear to be mistakenly labeled as "islands." Babylonian geographers made a similar error, suggesting that Gen. 10 reflects an ancient geographical convention.

133 D. W. Young. "The Influence of Babylonian Algebra on Longevity among the Antediluvians." *ZAW* 102 (1990): 321–35.

The chronological data in Gen. 5 reflects a familiarity with Babylonian sexagesimal mathematics. This is particularly visible in the prominence of certain numerical values, such as 10, 20, and 30, squares of these numbers, and the number 800.

134 G. A. Rendsburg. "The Internal Consistency and Historical Reliability of the Biblical Genealogies." *VT* 40 (1990): 185–206.

Contrary to common trends, concludes that the genealogies of the Pentateuch are historically reliable.

135 Y. B. Tsirkin. "Japheth's Progeny and the Phoenicians." Pp.

117–34 in *Phoenicia and the Bible.* Edited by E. Lipinski. OLA 44, Studia Phoenicia 11. Louvain: Peeters, 1991.

The author of Gen. 10 (the "Table of Nations") derived portions of his information from Phoenician sources during the first half of the seventh century B.C.E.

136 D. V. Etz. "The Numbers of Genesis v 3–31: A Suggested Conversion and Its Implications." *VT* 43 (1993): 171–89.

The long patriarchal lifespans in Gen. 5 differ in the MT, LXX, and Samaritan Pentateuch. Moreover, the numbers in 26 of 27 cases end in 0, 2, 5, or 7, which cannot be random (probability = 0.00073×10^{-6}). Etz concludes that the original lifespans were plausible and suggests a formula for making the conversions.

✓ **137** R. S. Hess. *Studies in the Personal Names of Genesis 1–11.* AOAT 234. Kevalaer, Germany: Butzon & Bercker; Neukirchen-Vluyn: Neukirchener, 1993.

Names in the genealogies of Gen. 1–11 fit a second-millennium B.C.E. context in the Upper Euphrates region. This suggests that these materials also originated during that period.

138 D. M. Carr. "Βιβλος γενεσεως Revisited: A Synchronic Analysis of Patterns in Genesis as Part of the Torah (Part One)." *ZAW* 110 (1998): 159–72; "Βιβλος γενεσεως Revisited: A Synchronic Analysis of Patterns in Genesis as Part of the Torah (Part Two)." *ZAW* 110 (1998): 327–47.

Explores the interrelationship between diachronic and synchronic aspects of the Genesis genealogies. Concludes that the genealogies provide the structure of Genesis as well as a genealogical prologue to the rest of the Pentateuch. Human beings are presented as the descendants of "heaven and earth" according to this scheme. Three genealogical structures comprise the entire Pentateuch: (1) Adam/Eve to the flood; (2) Noah to post-flood humanity; (3) Abraham to his Israelite progeny.

4.3.3 Interpreting Genesis 1–11

139 B. K. Waltke. *Creation and Chaos: An Exegetical and Theological Study of Biblical Cosmogony.* Portland, Oregon: Western Conservative Baptist Seminary, 1974.

Gen. 1 intends us to envision an initial chaos from which God created the universe. Hence, the initial phrase, "In the beginning, God created the heavens and the earth," is a title rather than the first act of creation. [For a critical response, see M. F. Rooker, "Genesis 1:1–3: Creation or Re-creation?" *BSac* 149 (1992): 316–23; "Genesis 1:1–3: Creation or Re-creation? (Part 2)," *BSac* 149 (1992): 411–27.]

140 G. J. Wenham. "The Coherence of the Flood Narrative." *VT* 28 (1978): 336–48.

  The flood story of Gen. 6–9 is a coherent and unified narrative. Although this does not preclude the presence of P and J sources in the story, it does raise questions about the validity of the source-critical approach.

141 D. J. A. Clines. "The Significance of the 'Sons of God' Episode (Genesis 6:1–4) in the Context of the 'Primeval History' (Genesis 1–11)." *JSOT* 13 (1979): 33–46.

  Although Gen. 6:1–4 may have originated as a separate piece of mythology, in its present context the episode has been carefully integrated into the primeval history, where it seems to promise a 120-year respite before the flood's arrival.

142 N. Wyatt. "Interpreting the Creation and Fall Story in Gen 2–3." *ZAW* 93 (1981): 10–21.

  The story of Gen. 2–3 was composed as a parable of the Israelite monarchy's fall to Assyria; the tale was later applied to Judah's fall at the hands of Babylon.

143 B. Lang. "Non-Semitic Deluge Stories and the Book of Genesis: A Bibliographical and Critical Survey." *Anthropos* 80 (1985): 604–16.

  Surveys non-Semitic evidence from around the world regarding flood traditions. Concludes that the wide distribution of flood stories among human societies does not reflect the antiquity and authenticity of the biblical flood tradition. Similarities between biblical and non-Semitic flood stories are the result of missionary influence.

144 N. Poulssen. "Time and Place in Genesis V." Pp. 21–33 in *Prophets, Worship, and Theodicy: Studies in Prophetism, Biblical Theology, and Structural and Rhetorical Analysis and on the Place of Music in Worship.* OtSt 24. Leiden: Brill, 1986.

  The conceptions of time offered by J and P in the primeval history are quite different. P's history follows linear contours while J views human history as cyclical and ongoing.

145 B. K. Waltke. "Cain and His Offering." *WTJ* 48 (1986): 363–72.

  God did not reject Cain's offering in Gen. 4 because it was bloodless. He rejected it because of Cain's heart, which moved him to feign worship with his offering. This motive contrasted with Abel's offering through faith.

146 J. A. Emerton. "An Examination of Some Attempts to Defend the Unity of the Flood Narrative in Genesis." *VT* 37 (1987): 401–20; "An Examination of Some Attempts to De-

fend the Unity of the Flood Narrative in Genesis, Part II."
VT 38 (1988): 1–21.

Two articles that critique recent attempts to argue, against the two-source (J and P) consensus, that the flood story is the work of a single author. Concludes that these efforts are misguided and generally careless.

147 R. S. Hendel. "Of Demigods and the Deluge: Towards an Interpretation of Genesis 6:1–4." *JBL* 106 (1987): 13–26.

Contrary to one common viewpoint, the *nephalim* text in Genesis 6:1–4 is not an isolated fragment or late addition to Genesis. Rather, it is an older tradition that J has taken up and integrated carefully into his history.

148 R. S. Hendel. "When the Sons of God Consorted with the Daughters of Men." *BRev* 3, no. 2 (1987): 8–13, 37.

The cohabitation of the divine *nephalim* with human women provided the original motive for the flood in Israelite tradition. J took up this tradition but added 6:5–8 in order to fit this *nephalim* text into a more general pattern of human evil, which was for J the reason for the flood.

149 R. W. L. Moberly. "Did the Serpent Get It Right?" *JTS* 39 (1988): 1–27.

This is the central problem of the fall story: Yahweh told Adam and Eve that they would die if they consumed the forbidden fruit, but the serpent deceived Eve with the words, "Surely you will not die"—and she did not. The solution is that the deaths of Adam and Eve were metaphorical rather than literal.

150 L. M. Barré. "The Riddle of the Flood Chronology." *JSOT* 41 (1988): 3–20.

Explores the flood chronologies of J and P. Concludes that J and P offer coherent but independent chronological systems for the flood. This suggests that the two accounts originated separately and were later joined by a redactor.

151 D. M. L. Judisch. "The Length of the Days of Creation." *CTQ* 52 (1988): 265–71.

The suggestion that the days of creation in Gen. 1 are actually "ages" (day-age theory) seeks to adapt the text to evolutionary theory. But neither the text, nor the ancients who wrote it, would have imagined such an idea. Gen. 1 speaks only of ordinary days.

152 D. T. Tsumura. *The Earth and the Waters in Genesis 1 and 2.* JSOTSup 83. Sheffield: JSOT, 1989.

The depictions of water in the two creation stories of Gen. 1–2 are compatible and hence reflect the concepts of a single cosmology.

153 J. P. Lewis. "The Days of Creation: An Historical Survey of Interpretation." *JETS* 32 (1989): 433–55.

Surveys Judaic and Christian interpretations of the creation days in Gen. 1–2 from the turn of the era until 1856.

154 J. M. Kennedy. "Peasants in Revolt: Political Allegory in Genesis 2–3." *JSOT* 47 (1990): 3–14.

The "creation-fall" of Gen. 2–3 is not a rendering of origins but rather a political allegory that incarnates the social and economic values of Israel's monarchic elite. The authority of the state is represented by the deity, while Adam and Eve represent peasants who are punished for their rebellion.

155 G. Wenham. "Original Sin in Genesis 1–11." *Churchman* 104 (1990): 309–21.

Genesis understands the primeval events of chapters 1–11 to have permanent results in creation and human life. Hence, these events are not merely paradigmatic but must be understood as historical on some level.

156 Y. Amit. "Biblical Utopianism: A Mapmaker's Guide to Eden." *USQR* 44 (1990): 11–17.

The Edenic garden of Gen. 2 is a literary utopian vision rather than the author's historical picture of early human life.

157 G. Green. "Myth, History, and Imagination: The Creation Narratives in Bible and Theology." *HBT* 12, no. 2 (1990): 19–38.

Karl Barth identified the creation stories of Genesis as inspired "guesses" about what must have preceded knowable reality. The constitutive element behind these narratives was therefore the human imagination.

158 R. S. Hess. "Genesis 1–2 in Its Literary Context." *TynBul* 41 (1990): 143–53.

The creation stories of Gen. 1 and 2 are juxtaposed in a manner similar to other materials in the primeval history of Gen. 1–11. Because this conforms to the literary pattern in chapters 1–11, there is no reason to presuppose that they stem from different sources.

√ **159** B. F. Batto. "Paradise Reexamined." Pp. 33–59 in *The Biblical Canon in Comparative Perspective: Scripture in Context VI*. Edited by K. L. Younger, Jr., W. W. Hallo, and B. F. Batto. Ancient Near Eastern Texts and Studies 11. Lewiston, N.Y.: Edwin Mellen, 1991.

J's "paradise-fall" story (Gen. 2–3) actually depicts an inchoate world and an emerging humanity. The paradise theme emerged only when the text was read alongside P's later creation story in Gen. 1. The common notion that Gen. 2–3 borrowed the paradise theme from a Near Eastern source is a misnomer, for no such theme existed in the Mesopotamian traditions.

160 T. D. Alexander. "Are the Wife/Sister Incidents of Genesis Literary Compositional Variants?" *VT* 42 (1992): 145–53.

Scholarship commonly assumes that the three wife/sister stories in Gen. 12, 20, and 26 are variants of the same story, with Gen. 12 being subsequently developed in the other two. Alexander argues against this and attributes all three stories to J.

161 L. A. Turner. "The Rainbow as the Sign of the Covenant in Genesis IX 11–13." *VT* 43 (1993): 119–24.

Like circumcision (Gen. 17) and Sabbath (Exod. 31:13–15), the rainbow of Gen. 9 symbolizes God's covenant, in this case with humanity. The rainbow's shape reflects the contours of the firmament, which failed and allowed the flood but which now, by God's promise, will never fail again.

162 R. S. Hess. "The Roles of the Woman and the Man in Genesis 3." *Them* 18, no. 3 (1993): 15–19.

The fall and its consequences (Gen. 3) depict the realities of Iron Age agricultural life rather than theological norms for gender roles.

163 J. Galambush. " *'ādām* from *'ădāmâ*, *'iššâ* from *'îš*: Derivation and Subordination in Genesis 2:4b–3:24." Pp. 33–46 in *History and Interpretation: Essays in Honour of John H. Hayes*. JSOTSup 173. Sheffield: JSOT, 1993.

Studies the terminology used in the creation/fall sequence of Gen. 2–3. The text reflects a narrative that simultaneously accounts for both the domination/subordination characteristic of marital relationships as well as the potential for mutuality. The text is merely etiological and suggests no remedy for this situation.

164 S. L. Jaki. "The Sabbath-Rest of the Maker of All." *AsTJ* 50 (1995): 37–49.

The seven-day creation of Gen. 1 was composed as a parable in which the deity served as a role model for keeping the Sabbath law.

165 J. Blenkinsopp. "P and J in Genesis 1:1–11:26: An Alternative Hypothesis." Pp. 1–15 in *Fortunate the Eyes That See: Essays in Honor of David Noel Freedman in Celebration of His Seventieth Birthday*. Edited by A. B. Beck. Grand Rapids: Eerdmans, 1995.

The primeval history of Gen. 1–11 was composed by P and later supplemented by the wisdom reflections of J. This reverses the usual order, which has P follow J.

166 G. A. Herion. "Why God Rejected Cain's Offering: The Obvious Answer." Pp. 52–65 in *Fortunate the Eyes That See: Essays in Honor of David Noel Freedman in Celebration*

of *His Seventieth Birthday*. Edited by A. B. Beck. Grand
Rapids: Eerdmans, 1995.
> God rejected Cain's offering in Gen. 4 because it came from the
> ground cursed in Gen. 3.

167 N. Cohn. *Noah's Flood: The Genesis Story in Western
Thought*. New Haven: Yale University Press, 1996.
> Surveys two millennia of tradition and interpretation related to
> the flood tradition of Genesis.

168 D. A. Sterchi. "Does Genesis 1 Provide a Chronological Sequence?" *JETS* 39 (1996): 529–36.
> The sequence of events in Gen. 1 is arranged primarily accord-
> ing to content rather than strict chronology, but this does not
> preclude that chronology played a role in the text's composition.

169 A. York. "The Maturation Theme in the Adam and Eve
Story." Pp. 393–410 in *"Go to the Land I Will Show You":
Studies in Honor of Dwight S. Young*. Edited by J. E. Coleson and V. H. Matthews. Winona Lake, Ind.: Eisenbrauns,
1996.
> In Gen. 3, Adam and Eve chose the knowledge of good and evil
> instead of immortality. In J's view, this was an expression of
> maturity. Only later did P and postbiblical Judaism portray this
> event as a tragic "fall."

170 E. Otto. "Die Paradieserzählung Genesis 2–3: Eine nach-
priesterschriftliche Lehrerzählung in ihrem religionshis-
torischen Kontext." Pp. 167–92 in *"Jedes Ding hat seine
Zeit . . .": Studien zur israelitischen und altorientalischen
Weisheit: Diethelm Michel zum 65. Geburtstag*. BZAW
241. Berlin and New York: de Gruyter, 1996.
> Contrary to the standard view, argues that the creation/fall in
> Gen. 2–3 is a supplement to Gen. 1 designed to explain the ori-
> gins of evil.

171 J. H. Tigay. "He Begot a Son in His Likeness after His
Image." Pp. 139–48 in *Tehillah le-Moshe: Biblical and Ju-
daic Studies in Honor of Moshe Greenberg*. Edited by
M. Cogan, B. L. Eichler, and J. H. Tigay. Winona Lake, Ind.:
Eisenbrauns, 1997.
> Birth anomalies were omens of evil in the ancient world. The
> comment that Adam begat a son "in his likeness and image"
> (Gen. 5:3) reflected the birth of a normal child and, therefore,
> confirmed God's covenant blessing.

172 P. H. Seely. "The Geographical Meaning of 'Earth' and
'Seas' in Genesis 1:10." *WTJ* 59 (1997): 231–55.
> The Old Testament presumes the ancient view of the cosmos,

namely, that the earth was a flat surface between primeval waters and a domed sky.

173 C. Scholten. "Weshalb wird die Schöpfungsgeschichte zum naturwissenschaftlichen Bericht?" *TQ* 177 (1997): 1–15.

Christian interpretations of the Genesis cosmologies followed two paths. One paradigm attempted to correlate Scripture with contemporary cosmological ideas (e.g., St. Basil, John Philiponon of Alexandria), while the other attempted to build a cosmology on Scripture alone (e.g., the Antiochene school; i.e., Gregory of Nyssa, Chrysostom, and Diodorus of Tarsus). This second paradigm resulted in a two-story square cosmology in which the first heaven was in the upper part of the lower story and the second heaven was a vaulted upper story.

174 K. Jeppesen. "What Was Created in the Beginning?" Pp. 59–65 in *"Lasset uns Brücken bauen . . .": Collected Communications to the XVth Congress of the Organization for the Study of the Old Testament, Cambridge 1995.* Frankfurt am Main: Lang, 1998.

The phrase "In the beginning God created the heavens and the earth" in Gen. 1:1 refers only to the creative activity of God in Gen. 1:2–10, that is, to the first three creation acts accomplished during the first two and one-half creation days.

175 M. D. Futato. "Because It Had Rained: A Study of Gen 2:5–7 with Implications for Gen 2:4–25 and Gen 1:1–2:3." *WTJ* 60 (1998): 1–21.

With respect to vegetation and humanity, the stories in Gen. 1 and Gen. 2:4–25 are arranged topically rather than chronologically. Moreover, the nearest Near Eastern counterparts to this tradition are Canaanite rather than Mesopotamian.

176 R. S. Hendel. *The Text of Genesis 1–11: Textual Studies and Critical Edition.* Oxford: Oxford University Press, 1998.

A detailed discussion of the text of Gen. 1–11 along with a critical edition that provides "an approximation to the original [text] insofar as that is reasonable" (114). Includes especially good discussions of the genealogies in Gen. 1–11.

177 P. J. Harland. "Vertical or Horizontal: The Sin of Babel." *VT* 48 (1998): 515–33.

In the context of J, the Babel story serves as one of several stories that illustrate the hubris of humanity. When read in the context of P, however, the sin of humanity at Babel was its resistance to the dispersion necessary to fulfill the divine command to multiply and "fill the earth."

178 M. H. Narrowe. "Another Look at the Tree of Good and Evil." *JBQ* 26 (1998): 184–88.

The "good and evil" of the garden tree is not a merism denoting the wholeness of human understanding. Rather, the tree of the knowledge of good and evil provided a divine excuse for banishing humanity from a spiritually repressive paradise.

179   J. Barr. " 'Was Everything That God Created Really Good?' A Question in the First Verse of the Bible." Pp. 55–65 in *God in the Fray: A Tribute to Walter Brueggemann.* Edited by T. Linafelt and T. K. Beal. Minneapolis: Fortress, 1998.

There are three possible interpretations of Gen. 1:1, "In the beginning God created the heavens and the earth." These include: (1) an initial act of creation prior to the creation of light on day one; (2) a temporal expression meaning, "in the beginning of God's creating heaven and earth"; (3) a statement that summarizes what God is about to do in his six days of creation. Barr suggests that the third option is far better than the other two.

180   T. A. Lenchak. "Puzzling Passages: 'So the Lord Put a Mark on Cain, Lest Anyone Should Kill Him at Sight' (Gen 4:15)." *TBT* 38 (2000): 53.

The protective mark that Cain received upon his banishment from Yahweh's presence reflects divine mercy and grace in the context of divine justice.

181   M. Witte. *Die biblische Urgeschichte: Redaktions- und theologiegeschichtliche Beobachtungen zu Genesis 1,1–11,26.* BZAW 265. Berlin and New York: de Gruyter, 1998.

The primeval history was submitted to a post-P redaction that sought to mediate between the older materials in J and P. This post-P redactor reflects all of the ideas prevalent in postexilic Judaism, including wisdom, Priestly, prophetic, and Deuteronomistic ideologies.

182   A. Pinker. "Nimrod Found?" *JBQ* 26 (1998): 237–45.

The ancient hero Nimrod, mentioned in Gen. 10:8–12, is none other than the god Marduk, head of the Babylonian pantheon. The linguistic development that accounts for this name change was MRDK to MRDN to NMRD.

183   J. Barr. "Adam: Single Man or Humanity?" Pp. 3–12 in *Hesed VeEmet: Studies in Honor of Ernest S. Frerichs.* Edited by J. Magness and S. Gitin. BJS 320. Atlanta: Scholars, 1998.

Explores the question of whether *adam* in the creation of Genesis refers to "humankind" or to an individual named "Adam." Argues that in Gen. 2 *adam* refers to an individual while in Gen. 1 it probably refers to humanity.

184   P. Swiggers. "Babel and the Confusion of Tongues (Gen 11:1–9)." Pp. 182–95 in *Mythos im Alten Testament und seiner Umwelt: Festschrift für Has-Peter Müller zum 65.*

Geburtstag. Edited by A. Lange et al. BZAW 278. Berlin: de Gruyter, 1999.

> Explores various compositional and interpretive aspects of the Babel story in Gen. 11.

185 W. A. M. Beuken. "The Human Person in the Vision of Genesis 1–3: A Synthesis of Contemporary Insights." *LB* 24 (1999): 3–20.

> The divine image in humanity is neither ontological nor psychological; it is functional. The human function is to maintain the divine creation by exercising authority and by filling the earth through procreation.

186 K. E. Greene-McCreight. *Ad Litteram: How Augustine, Calvin, and Barth Read the "Plain Sense" of Genesis 1–3.* Issues in Systematic Theology 5. Frankfurt am Main: Lang, 1999.

> As the title suggests, this volume addresses the history of the interpretation of Gen. 1–3.

187 M. G. Brett. "Politics of Identity: Reading Genesis in the Persian Period." *ABR* 47 (1999): 1–15.

> Combines historical and narratological approaches to Genesis and shows that the book is best understood as a polemic against the nationalistic and ethnocentric policies of the Ezra/Nehemiah reforms.

188 K. L. Sparks. "The Problem of Myth in Ancient Historiography." Pp. 269–80 in *Rethinking the Foundations: Historiography in the Ancient World and in the Bible (Essays in Honour of John Van Seters).* Edited by S. L. McKenzie and T. Römer. BZAW 294. Berlin and New York: de Gruyter, 2000.

> J composed the paradise/fall story of Gen. 2:4b–3:24 as a metaphorical myth by combining various motifs and themes from ancient texts and traditions. Hence, J viewed his myth as allegorical rather than historical.

189 T. Stordalen. *Echoes of Eden: Genesis 2–3 and Symbolism of the Eden Garden in Biblical Hebrew Literature.* CBET 25. Louvain: Peeters, 2000.

> Contrary to the recent tendency to date the paradise/fall in Gen. 2–3 late, Stordalen argues that these materials are not only early but also have exerted considerable influence on the Hebrew Bible and its theology.

190 R. Ouro. "The Earth of Genesis 1:2: Abiotic or Chaotic, Part I." *AUSS* 35 (1998): 259–76; "The Earth of Genesis 1:2: Abiotic or Chaotic, Part II." *AUSS* 37 (1999): 39–54;

"The Earth of Genesis 1:2: Abiotic or Chaotic, Part III."
AUSS 38 (2000): 59–67.

> Israel's cosmogony in Gen. 1:2 is unique and contrasts sharply
> with Mesopotamian cosmogonies.

191 J. A. Atwell. "An Egyptian Source for Genesis 1." *JTS* 51
(2000): 441–77.

> Gen. 1 reflects stronger influences from Egyptian cosmogonic
> traditions than from Mesopotamian exemplars like *Enuma Elish.*

192 R. W. L. Moberly. "Why Did Noah Send Out a Raven?" *VT*
50 (2000): 345–56.

> The raven's "back and forth" flight pattern above the waters in
> Gen. 8:6–7 mimics God's action in 8:1 by which the waters re-
> cede. This reflects P's preoccupations with *imitatio Dei.*

193 M. Emmrich. "The Temptation Narrative of Genesis 3:1–6:
A Prelude to the Pentateuch and the History of Israel."
EvQ 73 (2001): 3–20.

> The final form of the fall narrative reflects influences from the
> Deuteronomistic History and was composed to interpret the
> historical experiences of Israel.

194 K. A. D. Smelik. "The Creation of Sabbath (Gen 1:1–2:3)."
Pp. 9–11 in *Unless Someone Guides Me: Fs Karel A. Deur-
loo.* Edited by J. W. Dyk et al. ACEBTSup 2. Maastricht, the
Netherlands: Shaker, 2001.

> The creation of story of Gen. 1 is not a foreign composition ap-
> propriated by Israel, as is sometimes claimed, but is instead a
> uniquely Israelite composition whose chief concern is the ori-
> gin of the Sabbath.

4.4 The Patriarchs: Genesis 12–50

The divine promises to the patriarchs and Abraham's
covenant with the deity serve as foundational elements in most
Jewish and Christian theologies. While these themes provide a
coherent shape for the patriarchal narratives, behind this literary
and theological veneer stand a variety of older traditions and
compositions. For this reason compositional and source-critical
questions have played important roles in the study of these narratives. One important generic distinction in the patriarchal narratives is that scholars generally view the Joseph story in Gen.
37–50 as an independent novella that was subsequently included
in the Book of Genesis. By way of contrast, the Abraham-Isaac-
Jacob cycles are collections of short episodes rather than longer,
thematically unified stories.

4.4.1 General Discussions

195 A. Alt. *Der Gott der Väter: Ein Beitrag zur Vorgeschichte der israelitischen Religion.* BWANT 12. Stuttgart: Kohlhammer, 1929. English translation: "The God of the Fathers." Pp. 3–100 in *Essays on Old Testament History and Religion* by A. Alt. Garden City, N.Y.: Doubleday, 1968.

Various local El numina (e.g., El Elyon, El Shaddai, etc.) and their sacred sites became associated with the patriarchal family deities (gods of the fathers), which were in turn absorbed into the radically monotheistic religion of Moses. [F. M. Cross attempted to refine Alt's work on pp. 3–75 of *Canaanite Myth and Hebrew Epic* (#82). For a critical response to Alt, see J. Van Seters, "The Religion of the Patriarchs in Genesis," *Bib* 61 (1980): 220–33.]

196 W. F. Albright. "The Patriarchal Background of Israel's Faith." Pp. 53–109 in *Yahweh and the Gods of Canaan.* London: School of Oriental and African Studies, 1968. Reprint, Winona Lake, Ind.: Eisenbrauns, 1990.

The world described in the patriarchal narratives of Genesis coheres nicely with the second-millennium context and culture of the Near East.

197 T. L. Thompson. *The Historicity of the Patriarchal Narratives: The Quest for the Historical Abraham.* BZAW 133. Berlin: de Gruyter, 1974.

Archaeological data and the internal evidence of Genesis suggest that the patriarchal narratives are not historical compositions. [For a response to critiques of this work, see T. L. Thompson, "The Background of the Patriarchs: A Reply to William Dever and Malcolm Clark," *JSOT* 9 (1978): 2–43.]

198 J. Van Seters. *Abraham in History and Tradition.* New Haven: Yale University Press, 1975.

The Abraham story is the literary and theological composition of an exilic Yahwist and reflects few ancient traditions.

199 C. Westermann. *Die Verheissungen an die Väter: Studien zur Vätergeschichte.* FRLANT 116. Göttingen: Vandenhoeck & Ruprecht, 1976. English translation: *The Promises to the Fathers: Studies on the Patriarchal Narratives.* Philadelphia: Fortress, 1980.

Collects important essays by Westermann on the theme of the patriarch. Among the more important conclusions is that the patriarchal stories are not primarily etiological but instead reflect data from Israel's ancestral period. Westermann attempts to sift out these early materials through a form-critical study of the promises made by God to the forefathers.

200 S. M. Warner. "The Patriarchs and the Extra-biblical Sources." *JSOT* 2 (1977): 50–61.

Concludes that the studies of T. L. Thompson and J. Van Seters (#197; #198) have rendered untenable the Albright synthesis that supported the historicity of the patriarchs.

201 W. McKane. *Studies in the Patriarchal Narratives.* Edinburgh: Handsel, 1979.

Addresses matters of genre, tradition history, patriarchal religion, and theology. Numerous suggestions and theses are offered along the way, but the volume is essentially a survey of modern scholarship on the patriarchs.

202 T. Frymer-Kensky. "Patriarchal Family Relationships and Near Eastern Law." *BA* 44 (1981): 209–14.

A comparison of the patriarchal narratives with the legal traditions and cultural milieu of ancient Mesopotamia suggests the historical plausibility and authenticity of the biblical narrative.

203 J. A. Emerton. "The Origin of the Promises to the Patriarchs in the Older Sources of the Book of Genesis." *VT* 32 (1982): 14–32.

Distinguishes an original layer of promises to the patriarchs from later developments of this theme.

204 A. R. Millard and D. J. Wiseman, eds. *Essays on the Patriarchal Narratives.* Winona Lake, Ind.: Eisenbrauns, 1983.

Addresses a growing skepticism about the historicity of the patriarchs and patriarchal age by offering a more positive assessment of the evidence. Taken together, the studies argue that the evidence does indeed support the historicity of the patriarchal narratives and their setting in the second millennium B.C.E.

205 U. Worschech. *Abraham: Eine sozialgeschichtliche Studie.* Frankfurt: Lang, 1983.

When read in light of the sociology of West Semitic pastoralism, the Abraham traditions appear to be historically accurate portrayals of a pastoral nomad. [For an English review, see B. Halpern, *BASOR* 275 (1989): 77–79.]

206 Z. Weisman. "Diverse Historical and Social Reflections in the Shaping of Patriarchal History." *Zion* 50 (1985): 1–13.

The Jacob traditions stem from a different context than, and are older than, those of Abraham and Isaac. E's version represents the oldest layer of the Jacob tradition and J was responsible for the composition that combined E with the Abraham and Isaac traditions.

207 R. K. Harrison. "Philistine Origins: A Reappraisal." Pp. 11–19 in *Ascribe to the Lord: Biblical and Other Studies in Memory of Peter C. Craigie.* Edited by L. Eslinger and G. Taylor. JSOTSup 67. Sheffield: Sheffield Academic Press, 1988.

> References to the Philistines in Genesis are commonly taken as evidence that the text or traditions are much later then any supposed primeval or patriarchal age. However, the "Philistines" to which these texts refer were the Casluhim peoples of the third millennium B.C.E.

208 N. Steinberg. "Alliance or Descent? The Function of Marriage in Genesis." *JSOT* 51 (1991): 45–55.

> Marriage in Gen. 12–36 functions to establish patrilineal descent in the family of Terah rather than to form strategic alliances.

209 R. S. Hess, ed. *He Swore an Oath: Biblical Themes from Genesis 12–50.* 2d ed. Grand Rapids: Baker, 1994.

> A collection of ten evangelical essays addressing various aspects of the patriarchal narratives.

210 J. Strange. "Geography and Tradition in the Patriarchal Narratives." *SJOT* 11 (1997): 210–22.

> Attempts to use geography as a key to unravel the tradition history of the patriarchal traditions. Among other things, concludes that the Jacob/Joseph traditions originated in the north while Abraham/Isaac traditions originated in the south.

4.4.2 The Abraham-Isaac Story: Interpreting Genesis 12–25

The reader will notice that Isaac is here combined with Abraham's story. This is a matter of convenience, for Isaac also plays a role in the Jacob story that follows. What should be noted is that, essentially, there is no "Isaac story" in Genesis so much as we have Isaac playing roles in the Abraham and then the Jacob narratives. The collection of independent Isaac stories is found in Gen. 26, and it is interesting that these stories are in every case reflections of the Abraham story. Some scholars therefore conclude that the Isaac story was constructed on the basis of the older Abraham story (see Van Seters [#198]), probably because the author did not have sources for his history of Isaac.

211 R. E. Clements. *Abraham and David: Genesis XV and Its Meaning for Israelite Tradition.* Naperville, Ill.: Allenson, 1967.

> Why the paucity of references to Abraham outside of the Pentateuch? Abraham's ancient covenant tradition was connected

with Hebron, from which David took it to his new capital in Jerusalem. There it was absorbed into the Davidic covenant. Formal and thematic similarities between the Abrahamic and Davidic covenants provide support for this conclusion.

212 D. Irvin. *Mytharion: The Comparison of Tales from the Old Testament and the Ancient Near East*. AOAT 32. Neukirchen-Vluyn: Neukirchener Verlag, 1978.

Compares several stories in the patriarchal narratives (Gen. 16, 18–19, 21, 22, and 28) with myths and tales from the Near East.

213 N.-E. Andreasen. "Genesis 14 in Its Near Eastern Context." Pp. 59–77 in *Scripture in Context: Essays on the Comparative Method*. Edited by C. D. Evans, W. W. Hallo, and J. B. White. Pittsburgh: Pickwick, 1980.

Some scholars view the battle on the plain in Gen. 14 as an ancient historical tradition and others as a late, midrashic fabrication. This article concludes that the text is a historiographic narrative that attempts to narrate the past, but the source and date of the information used by the historian cannot be easily ascertained, nor can the historicity of the tradition.

214 T. D. Alexander. "Genesis 22 and the Covenant of Circumcision." *JSOT* 25 (1983): 17–22.

The sacrifice of Isaac in Gen. 22 represents the ratification ceremony for the covenant of circumcision in Gen. 17.

215 S. Lasine. "Guest and Host in Judges 19: Lot's Hospitality in an Inverted World." *JSOT* 29 (1984): 37–59.

An intertextual study of two very similar episodes in Gen. 19 and Judg. 19.

216 L. Katzoff. "From the Nuzi Tablets." *Dor le Dor* 13 (1985): 216–19.

Abraham's claim that Sarah was his sister, his adoption of Eliezer as an heir, and his acceptance of Hagar's child in lieu of Sarah's are all customs reflected in Hurrian society.

217 H.-C. Schmitt. "Die Erzählung von der Versuch Abrahams Gen 22, 1–19* und das Problem einer Theologie der elohistischen Pentateuchtexts." *BN* 34 (1986): 82–109.

Gen. 22 reflects the themes of temptation and the fear of God, as well as concern for the problem of human sacrifice. These three motifs reflect themes that were important for E in his northern context.

218 H. Gese. "Der auszulegende Text." *TQ* 167 (1987): 252–65.

Although Ishmael, according to the Genesis chronology, was more than fourteen years old, Gen. 21 portrays him playing with Isaac and has Hagar carry him away on her shoulder. Ancient scholars recognized these kinds of problems but, out of respect for tradition, preferred to preserve rather than harmonize.

219 J. Ha. *Genesis 15.* BZAW 181. Berlin and New York: de Gruyter, 1989.

The covenant with Abraham presented in Gen. 15 is a postexilic theological compendium that reflects familiarity with the earlier traditions of J, P, and D. [This supports the increasingly popular notion of a post-P redactor who created the Pentateuch (cf. Schmid [#65]).]

220 T. D. Alexander. "The Hagar Traditions in Genesis XVI and XXI. Pp. 131–48 in *Studies in the Pentateuch.* Edited by J. A. Emerton. VTSup 41. Leiden: E. J. Brill, 1990.

The Hagar tales in Gen. 16 and 21 are commonly viewed as doublets stemming from the J and E sources, respectively. However, there is no reason to view them as doublets nor is it helpful to view them as having been written by different authors.

221 J. A. Emerton. "Some Problems in Genesis XIV." Pp. 73–102 in *Studies in the Pentateuch.* Edited by J. A. Emerton. VTSup 41. Leiden: E. J. Brill, 1990.

Gen. 14 reflects several different layers of material, with the oldest dating before the time of David and the latest dating sometime after the seventh century B.C.E.

222 M. E. Biddle. "The 'Endangered Ancestress' and Blessing for the Nations." *JBL* 109 (1990): 599–611.

The three wife/sister stories in Gen. 12, 20, and 26 related to the blessing/curse theme of the patriarchal promise. The three stories explore how this aspect of the promise works out and come to somewhat different conclusions.

223 J. K. Hoffmeier. "The Wives' Tales of Genesis 12, 20, and 26 and the Covenants at Beer-sheba." *TynBul* 43 (1992): 81–99.

When compared to Near Eastern evidence, it appears that the wife/sister stories of Genesis reflect covenant-making conventions from the second millennium B.C.E.

224 I. N. Rashkow. "Intertextuality, Transference, and the Reader in/of Genesis 12 and 20." Pp. 57–73 in *Reading between Texts: Intertextuality and the Hebrew Bible.* Edited by D. N. Fewell. Louisville: Westminster John Knox, 1992.

The wife/sister story in Gen. 20 is commonly viewed as a composition designed to address theological ambiguities created by the earlier story in Gen. 12. Rashkow explores how the human tendency to transfer information from one episode to another makes such an effort effective.

225 A. Lemaire. "Cycle primitif d'Abraham et contexte géo-graphico-historique." Pp. 62–75 in *History and Tradition of Early Israel: Studies Presented to Eduard Nielsen*. Edited by A. Lemaire and B. Otzen. VTSup 50. Leiden: Brill, 1993.

A historically and geographically sensitive reading of the Abraham traditions suggests that the earliest cycle of tradition originated in the tenth-century environs of Hebron and in association with David's operations there. These traditions were orally composed and combined with other traditions (e.g., Lot, Ishmael, Isaac) in an effort to unify groups in the region around David.

226 R. S. Hess. "The Slaughter of the Animals in Genesis 15: Genesis 15:8–21 and Its Ancient Near Eastern Context." Pp. 55–65 in *He Swore an Oath: Biblical Themes from Genesis 12–50*. Edited by R. S. Hess. 2d ed. Grand Rapids: Baker, 1994.

The covenant ceremony in Gen. 15 is closer to practices reflected in second-millennium B.C.E. sources from Alalakh than to sources from the first-millennium Sefîre treaties and Jer. 34.

227 L. L. Lyke. "Where Does 'the Boy' Belong? Compositional Strategy in Genesis 21:14." *CBQ* 56 (1994): 637–48.

Gen. 21:14 depicts Abraham placing the infant Ishmael on his mother's (Hagar's) back. The unusual syntax, which placed *w't hyld* ("and the boy") at the end of the clause, was a matter of emphasis.

228 L. Teugels. "A Matriarchal Cycle? The Portrayal of Isaac in Genesis in the Light of the Presentation of Rebekah." *BTFT* 56 (1995): 61–72.

The brevity of the Isaac tradition in Genesis stems from the narrative's emphasis on Rebekah, whose strong character contrasts with Isaac's passive reception of the promise.

229 T. H. Hart. "Lot's Incest." *TBT* 33 (1995): 266–71.

The incestuous origins of Ammon and Moab (as progeny of Lot's daughters, impregnated by Lot) reflect a nationalistic agenda that mocked Israel's foreign neighbors.

230 J. A. Soggin. "Abraham and the Eastern Kings: On Genesis 14." Pp. 283–89 in *Solving Riddles and Untying Knots: Biblical, Epigraphic, and Semitic Studies in Honor of Jonas C. Greenfield*. Edited by Z. Zevit et al. Winona Lake, Ind.: Eisenbrauns, 1995.

Gen. 14 is a Hasmonean-era composition designed to legitimize either the Jerusalem priesthood or the Hasmonean kings through an appeal to the Melchizedek figure.

231 A. Wénin. "Abraham, election, et salut: Réflexions exégétiques et théologiques sur Genèse 12 dans son contexte narratif." *RTP* 27 (1996): 3–24.

Gen. 12 presents the ground rules by which Abraham's election serves its salvific role by blessing all nations. The nations are encouraged to recognize the election of Abraham's seed, while Abraham's seed is encouraged to avoid jealously protecting its election. The wife-sister story in 12:10–20 illustrates the principles stated in 12:1–9.

232 B. L. Eichler. "On Reading Genesis 12:10–20." Pp. 23–38 in *Tehillah le-Moshe: Biblical and Judaic Studies in Honor of Moshe Greenberg.* Edited by M. Cogan, B. L. Eichler, and J. H. Tigay. Winona Lake, Ind.: Eisenbrauns, 1997.

Employs structuralist narratology in a reading of the wife/sister story of Gen. 12. Concludes that Abram assumed the status of Sarai's brother because of the protective relationship this formed in the Near East and in order to save his own life.

233 W. W. Fields. *Sodom and Gomorrah: History and Motif in Biblical Literature.* JSOTSup 231. Sheffield: Sheffield Academic Press, 1997.

The narratives about Sodom and Gomorrah in Gen. 18–19 are didactic rather than historiographic.

234 T. Römer. "Qui est Abraham? Les différentes figures du patriarche dans la Bible hébraïque." Pp. 13–33 in *Abraham: Nouvelle jeunesse d'un ancêstre.* Edited by T. Römer. Essais bibliques 28. Geneva: Labor et Fides, 1997.

Portrayals of the forefather Abraham were adapted to address the particular concerns of Israelite communities at different points in history. These communities included exilic Judah, the returning exiles, postexilic priestly communities, and postexilic Diaspora Judaism.

235 D. B. Sharp. "On the Motherhood of Sarah: A Yahwistic Theological Comment." *IBS* 20 (1998): 2–14.

Sarah's attempt to have a son through Hagar was viewed by the Yahwist as a faithless act. Nevertheless, the Yahwist employed this tradition polemically to show that Yahweh rather than Baal had power over fertility.

236 J. Kirsch. "What Did Sarah See?" *BRev* 14, no. 5 (1998): 2, 49.

The "play" that Sarah saw with respect to Ishmael and Isaac in Gen. 21:9 was of a sexual nature. This explains Sarah's violent reaction to Ishmael and Hagar.

237 J. D. Levenson. "Abusing Abraham: Traditions, Religious
Histories, and Modern Misinterpretations." *Judaism* 47
(1998): 259–77.
>   Critiques efforts to characterize Abraham's sacrifice of Isaac as
>   either child abuse or as a negative commentary on the patri-
>   arch's character.

238 A. de Pury. "Abraham, the Priestly Writer's 'Ecumenical'
Ancestor." Pp. 163–81 in *Rethinking the Foundations:
Historiography in the Ancient World and in the Bible (Es-
says in Honour of John Van Seters)*. Edited by S. L. McKen-
zie and T. Römer. BZAW 294. Berlin and New York: de
Gruyter, 2000.
>   The Priestly writer was the first to link the primeval history
>   and patriarchs into a single narrative. This narrative presented
>   Abraham as an ecumenical ancestor for humanity, now recon-
>   ciled with Yahweh around his priestly people, Israel.

√ **239** P. R. Williamson. *Abraham, Israel, and the Nations: The
Patriarchal Promise and Its Covenantal Development in
Genesis*. JSOTSup 315. Sheffield: Sheffield Academic
Press, 2000.
>   Standard diachronic readings of Gen. 15 and Gen. 17 attribute
>   the two covenants to different literary strata. Williamson ar-
>   gues for a synchronic reading in which the covenant of Gen. 15
>   was contingent on Abraham's moral purity and Gen. 17 was
>   necessitated by the patriarch's failure to keep the moral
>   covenant.

4.4.3 The Jacob Story: Interpreting Genesis 26–35

The Jacob story poses numerous compositional, traditio-historical, literary, rhetorical, and theological questions. On a literary level, scholars are interested in how the various motifs and
episodes in the story relate to each other. Compositionally, there
is an ongoing debate about whether the author of Genesis composed the Jacob story or whether he simply took up an already
existing story and included it in his book. Among the important
traditio-historical questions is the development of the Jacob tradition as reflected in the Hebrew sources (see, for example, Good
[#240]; Whitt [#248]).

240 E. M. Good. "Hosea and the Jacob Tradition." *VT* 16 (1966):
137–51.
>   Hosea depicts a Jacob whose image was just becoming incorpo-
>   rated into the Yahwistic sphere. There was as yet no Yahwistic

story of Jacob, and Hosea's negative appraisal of Jacob suggests that the prophet wished it to stay that way.

241 V. H. Matthews and F. Mims. "Jacob the Trickster and Heir of the Covenant: A Literary Interpretation." *PRSt* 12 (1985): 185–95.

As in the Abraham and Isaac stories, a primary concern of the Jacob story is his effort to overcome every hurdle that shields him from inheriting the covenant. Through deception and cunning, he surmounted the obstacles of legal primogeniture (Esau was the older son) and in-law problems (conflicts with Laban). The audience of the text would have applauded the trickster character of their forefather with nationalistic fervor, for the victory of Jacob over Esau represented a victory of Israel over Edom.

242 A. P. Ross. "Jacob's Vision: The Founding of Bethel." *BSac* 142 (1985): 224–37; "Jacob at the Jabbok, Israel at Peniel." *BSac* 142 (1985): 338–54.

While fleeing Esau, Jacob became a true worshiper of Yahweh at Bethel. When Jacob returned to face Esau, God resisted the devious patriarch's return to the land but, after defeating Jacob, blessed him.

243 A. J. Heckelman. "Was Father Isaac a Co-conspirator?" *Dor le Dor* 13 (1985): 225–34.

Isaac co-conspired in the "deception" that granted Jacob the blessing because he saw that Esau was not suited for it.

244 R. E. Friedman. "Deception for Deception." *BRev* 2, no. 1 (1986): 22–31.

The Jacob cycle is constructed as a series of deceptions and conflicts (Jacob deceives Esau, Jacob and Rebekah deceive Isaac, Laban deceives Jacob, etc.). The cycle of deception ended when Joseph revealed his true identity to his brothers.

245 R. S. Hendel. *The Epic of the Patriarch: The Jacob Cycle and the Narrative Traditions of Canaan and Israel.* HSM 42. Atlanta: Scholars, 1987.

The Jacob story reflects a long pre-history as oral epic, as suggested by its internal features and by the motifs it shares with the Near Eastern epic traditions from Ugarit (Kirtu, Aqhat) and Mesopotamia (Gilgamesh).

246 K. Luke. "Esau's Marriage." *Indian Theological Studies* 25 (1988): 171–90.

In order to counter the threat posed by foreign marriages during the postexilic period, an author joined Esau's exclusion from the covenant promise with his marriage of foreign wives (Gen. 26:34).

247 S. A. Geller. "The Sack of Shechem: The Use of Typology in Biblical Covenant Religion." *Prooftexts* 10 (1990): 1–15.

The primary themes of the Shechem episode (Gen. 34) are the problem of exogamy (marriage with foreign Canaanites) and the prescription that all Canaanites must be exterminated. While this is merely a literary tradition, such a malevolent typology can potentially transition from archetype to reality, becoming dangerous in the process.

248 W. D. Whitt. "The Jacob Traditions in Hosea and Their Relation to Genesis." *ZAW* 103 (1991): 18–43.

A comparison of the Jacob traditions in Hosea with those in Genesis demonstrates that Hosea's portrait is the older of the two traditions, suggesting that Genesis was written later than Hosea (eighth century B.C.E.).

249 A. A. Keefe. "Rapes of Women/Wars of Men." *Semeia* 61 (1993): 79–97.

Explores the relationship between rape and war in three similar texts, Gen. 34, Judg. 19, and 2 Sam. 13.

250 L. M. Bechtel. "What if Dinah Is Not Raped? (Genesis 34)." *JSOT* 62 (1994): 16–36.

Dinah and Jacob reflect an openness to foreign relationships (e.g., with the Shechemites), while Levi and Simeon reflect xenophobic tendencies that the story portrays as dangerous. This implies, of course, that Dinah was not raped in Gen. 34.

251 F. Crüsemann. "Domination, Guilt, and Reconciliation: The Contribution of the Jacob Narrative in Genesis to Political Ethics." *Semeia* 66 (1994): 67–77.

The Jacob-Esau cycle is a commentary on the relationship between Israel and Edom. Israel must renounce its claim to supremacy over Edom in order to achieve reconciliation.

252 H. M. Wahl. *Die Jakobserzählungen: Studien zu ihrer mündlichen Überlieferung, Verschriftung und Historizität.* BZAW 258. Berlin and New York: de Gruyter, 1997.

The Jacob story was composed in the Judean royal courts just before the exile. The long process of oral tradition that preceded this composition precludes the possibility that the traditions preserve information about much earlier periods.

253 S. Scholz. *Rape Plots: A Feminist Cultural Study of Genesis 34.* Studies in Biblical Literature 13. New York: Lang, 2000.

Biblical scholarship has neglected the thematic importance of Dinah's rape in Gen. 34 and in doing so has contributed to the "rape culture" of the West.

254 J. Miles. "Jacob's Wrestling Match: Was It an Angel or Esau?" *BRev* 14, no. 5 (1998): 22–23.

The "man" whom Jacob wrestled in Gen. 32 was none other than Esau, as Jacob suggests when he meets Esau in Gen. 33:10: "for truly to see your [Esau's] face is like seeing the face of God."

255 T. E. Fretheim. "Which Blessing Does Isaac Give Jacob?" Pp. 279–91 in *Jews, Christians, and the Theology of the Hebrew Scriptures*. Edited by A. O. Bellis and J. S. Kaminsky. SBLSymS 8. Atlanta: Society of Biblical Literature, 2000.

Explores the themes of blessing and promise in Gen. 26:34–28:9, which contains Isaac's farewell blessing. The blessing does not pass to Jacob through the deception of Isaac but is instead received by Jacob at Bethel (Gen. 32).

256 D. Marcus. "Traditional Jewish Responses to the Question of Deceit in Genesis 27." Pp. 293–305 in *Jews, Christians, and the Theology of the Hebrew Scriptures*. Edited by A. O. Bellis and J. S. Kaminsky. SBLSymS 8. Atlanta: Society of Biblical Literature, 2000.

There are two common strategies among Jewish interpreters of Jacob's deception of Isaac. The moral strategy places the blame on Rebekah or Isaac, and the amoral strategy justifies Jacob's deception.

4.4.4 The Family of Esau:
Genealogies and Lists (Genesis 36 and Related Texts)

Genesis 36 is a collection of genealogical and list traditions regarding the family, leaders, and political rulers of Edom. For purposes of convenience, Bartlett's discussion of Edom in Israelite tradition is also included.

257 J. R. Bartlett. "The Edomite King-List of Genesis XXXVI. 31–39 and I Chron. I. 43–50." *JTS* 16 (1965): 314.

The Edomite king list in Gen. 36 reflects two different formulaic patterns when it refers to the place of rule or origin of the kings. When this pattern is correlated with geopolitical data, it becomes clear that the list was constructed by combining two older lists, one Moabite and the other Edomite. These sources go back to the eleventh or twelfth centuries B.C.E.

258 J. R. Bartlett. "The Brotherhood of Edom." *JSOT* 2 (1977): 2–27.

Israel's ideas about Edom developed in four phases, including Edom's subordination (Davidic period, see J and E), rebellion (see Amos and Num. 20), tolerance (see Deuteronomy), and extreme bitterness (see Obadiah, Malachi).

259 E. A. Knauf. "Alter und Herkunft der edomitischen Kö-
nigsliste Gen 36,31–39." *ZAW* 97 (1985): 245–53.
> Archaeological evidence and a study of its contents reveals that
> the Edomite king list of Gen. 36:31–39 reflects a context during
> the sixth or fifth centuries B.C.E.

4.4.5 The Joseph Story: Interpreting Genesis 37–50

Generically speaking, scholars usually view the Joseph story
as a novella. Although this tale provides the bridge between the
patriarchs and the Egyptian sojourn of Israel, there is some debate about whether it was composed for this purpose or taken up
and adapted for this purpose. Other matters of debate concern
the date of the story, its theology, and the potential presence of
sources in the text.

4.4.5.1 Composition, Authorship, and Context

260 G. von Rad. "Josephsgeschichte und ältere Chokma." Pp.
120–27 in *Congress Volume, Copenhagen, 1953.* VTSup 1.
Leiden: Brill, 1953. English translation: "The Joseph Narrative and Ancient Wisdom." Pp. 292–300 in *The Problem
of the Hexateuch and Other Essays.* London: Oliver and
Boyd, 1966.
> The Joseph story is best understood as a wisdom novella that
> reflects a high level of literary skill, subtlety in the presenta-
> tion of its characters, and a distinctive view of divine activity
> in human life. [Nevertheless, von Rad maintained the common
> source-critical theory of the story's origins (J + E) in his mono-
> graph *Die Josephserzählung.*]

261 R. N. Whybray. "The Joseph Story and Pentateuchal Criticism." *VT* 18 (1968): 522–28.
> Scholars tend to view the Joseph story as a novel of unique lit-
> erary quality as well as a text composed by joining sources from
> J and E. These two characterizations are incompatible and,
> given the story's coherence and literary genius, it is best to
> view the text as a novella and to reject source-critical theories
> of its origins.

262 D. B. Redford. *A Study of the Biblical Story of Joseph (Genesis 47–50).* VTSup 20. Leiden: Brill, 1970.
> The original Joseph story was composed, between the seventh
> and fifth centuries B.C.E., as an entertaining tale. Its "Egypt-
> ian" coloring is quite minimal and, where it is authentic, the
> connection is with late Egyptian tradition. Although the first

edition of the story gave prominence to Reuben, the tale was later edited to grant Judah this prominence. The editor of Genesis then took up this pro-Judah version and added it to his work.

263 G. W. Coats. *From Canaan to Egypt: Structural and Theological Context for the Joseph Story.* Washington, D.C.: Catholic Biblical Association, 1976.

The structural coherence of the Joseph story suggests that it was not composed from different parallel sources but is instead the work of a single author, perhaps J. The novella's primary themes include (1) the reconciliation of a family wherein all the parties—Joseph, father, and brothers—have played a role in creating alienation; and (2) the characteristics of an ideal administrator. Theologically, God is present behind the scenes as both themes develop.

264 H.-C. Schmitt. *Die Nichtpriesterliche Josephsgeschichte: Ein Beitrag zur neuesten Pentateuchkritik.* BZAW 154. Berlin and New York: de Gruyter, 1980.

The pre-Priestly Joseph story was composed in three stages. In the original version, an Ephraimite during the early Judean monarchy sought to cast the older northern Joseph traditions as an all-Israel story. Consequently, this *Judah-Schicht* emphasized the prominence of the royal tribe of Judah. The second layer of material, a *Ruben-Schicht*, was composed by the Elohist as a part of his composition that joined the patriarchal and exodus traditions and included an emphasis on the oldest of Jacob's sons, Reuben. This second layer was composed sometime between the late monarchy and early postexilic period. Finally, a *Jahwe-Schicht* was composed during the exilic or postexilic period, its emphasis being that Israel would be a blessing to all peoples. Therefore, with regard to the Pentateuch, its composition followed this path: smaller compositions were joined by an E redactor, and this composition was then edited by J and P.

265 W. Dietrich. *Die Josephserzählung als Novelle und Geschichtsschreibung: Zugleich ein Beitrag zur Pentateuchfrage.* Biblisch-theologische Studien 14. Neukirchen-Vluyn: Neukirchener Verlag, 1989.

The Joseph story originated as a northern novella that promoted northern identity soon after the split of the two Israelite kingdoms. A Judean editor later reworked this novella to create a bridge that joined the patriarchal and exodus traditions into a single narrative. This editor's concern was to provide a narrative heritage for future Israelites.

4.4.5.2 Interpreting the Joseph Story

266 K. Luke. "The Blessing Jacob Conferred upon Ephraim
(Gen 48:8–20)." *Irish Theological Studies* 14 (1977): 72–90.
Jacob's blessing reflects a context in which Ephraim gained
prominence over his brothers, which, according to Luke, must
have been during the Judges period.

267 H. Seebass. "The Joseph Story, Genesis 48, and the Canonical Process." *JSOT* 35 (1986): 29–53.
A synchronic and diachronic reading of Gen. 48 (blessing of
Ephraim and Manasseh) that attempts to assess as well the
text's role in the story of Joseph and the canonical process.

268 J. R. King. "The Joseph Story and Divine Politics: A Comparative Study of a Biographic Formula from the Ancient
Near East." *JBL* 106 (1987): 577–94.
The plot of the Joseph story follows a standard biographical format from the Near East. This "exile-reconciliation" pattern is
found in the Egyptian tale of Sinuhe, as well as in other Near
Eastern exemplars.

269 T. Chetwynd. "A Seven-Year Famine in the Reign of King
Djoser with Other Parallels between Imhotep and Joseph."
Catastrophism and Ancient History 9 (1987): 49–56.
Compares Egyptian traditions about a seven-year famine with
the similar element in the Joseph story. Suggests that Joseph is
best associated with the Egyptian Old Kingdom.

270 J. A. Soggin. "Notes on the Joseph Story." Pp. 336–49 in
*Understanding Poets and Prophets: Essays in Honour of
George Wishart Anderson*. Edited by A. G. Auld. JSOTSup
152. Sheffield: JSOT, 1993.
The Joseph story is a novella composed during the Seleucid pe-
riod (second century B.C.E.) to encourage persecuted Jews.

271 V. H. Matthews. "The Anthropology of Clothing in the
Joseph Narrative." *JSOT* 65 (1995): 25–36.
Clothing serves a significant role in signaling changes of status
and favor in the Joseph narrative. Jacob shows his preference for
Jacob with a special coat, Joseph loses this coat when he is sold
into slavery, Joseph receives a royal robe when Pharaoh grants
him prominence, and, at the story's conclusion, Joseph rewards
his brothers with new clothes, granting his favorite brother,
Benjamin, five sets of garments.

272 H. M. Wahl. "Das Motiv des 'Aufstiegs' in der Hofge-
schichte: Am Beispiel von Joseph, Esther und Daniel."
ZAW 112 (2000): 59–74.
The stories of Joseph, Esther, and Daniel reflect similar "court-

narrative" motifs in which a Jew rises to power in a foreign context. These stories address the particular problems and issues faced when Jews are in exile.

√ **273** Y.-W. Fung. *Victim and Victimizer: Joseph's Interpretation of His Destiny.* JSOTSup 308. Sheffield: Sheffield Academic Press, 2000.

This structuralist reading of the Joseph story explores the protagonist's character through a study of his speeches. Alongside the common theme of "fraternal strife" in the Joseph story stands one in which a slave makes a nation of slaves.

274 M. V. Fox. "Wisdom in the Joseph Story." *VT* 51 (2001): 26–41.

The Joseph story reflects wisdom influence, but not via the traditional ethical wisdom vis-à-vis Proverbs. The wisdom of the Joseph story is closer to the pietistic wisdom of the Book of Daniel.

4.4.5.3 Judah and Tamar: Genesis 38

This tale presents us with two primary problems. First, why does it appear to "interrupt" the Joseph story? Second, when, where, and why was the story written?

275 J. A. Emerton. "Judah and Tamar." *VT* 29 (1979): 403–15.

Gen. 38 originated as a Canaanite tradition that was critical of Judah. This story was subsequently adopted by Israelites and combined with their traditions.

276 G. A. Rendsburg. "David and His Circle in Genesis XXXVIII." *VT* 36 (1986): 438–46.

The story of Judah and Tamar was composed during the Davidic monarchy to entertain and to parody David's court. Hence, numerous correspondences exist between the characters of Gen. 38 and those associated with David's reign: Judah = David; Hirah = Hiram; daughters of Shua = Bathsheba; Selah = Solomon; Er = son of David/Bathsheba that perished; Tamar = Tamar; and so on.

277 J. L. Ska. "L'Ironie de Tamar (Gen 38)." *ZAW* 100 (1988): 261–63.

The story of Judah and Tamar effects irony in the reader through variations in the knowledge—and lack thereof—in the characters of the story and the reader. The text begins with Tamar knowing less than the characters or the reader, proceeds to bring Tamar to the same knowledge level, and then ends with Tamar's knowledge surpassing that of the characters and reader.

278 J. A. Soggin. "Judah and Tamar (Genesis 38)." Pp. 281–87 in

Of Prophets' Visions and the Wisdom of Sages: Essays in Honour of R. Norman Whybray on His Seventieth Birthday. Edited by H. A. McKay and D. J. A. Clines. JSOTSup 163. Sheffield: JSOT, 1993.

> The purpose of Gen. 38 is to provide a genealogy of King David while at the same time to stress the presence of Canaanite elements within the genealogy (Tamar). The text is difficult to date.

279 C. Y. S. Ho. "The Stories of the Family Troubles of Judah and David: A Study of Their Literary Links." *VT* 49 (1999): 514–31.

> The story of Judah and Tamar in Gen. 38 drew the names of its protagonists as well as its plot and theme from materials in the so-called Succession Narrative (2 Sam. 9–20, 1 Kings 1–2). Therefore, the story does not rest on any old oral or written traditions. The story was composed to link David with Judah through Perez (cf. Ruth 4:12–22).

280 J. Lambe. "Judah's Development: The Pattern of Departure-Transition-Return." *JSOT* 83 (1999): 53–68.

> The departure-transition-return pattern is visible both in the Judah/Tamar episode (Gen. 38) and in the Joseph story as a whole (Gen. 37–50). Hence, Gen. 38 should be understood as a part of, and not an interruption in, the Joseph story.

281 W. Warning. "Terminological Patterns and Genesis 38." *AUSS* 38 (2000): 293–305.

> The story of Judah and Tamar in Gen. 38 does not interrupt the story of Joseph in Gen. 37–50 but is instead an integral part of the Joseph cycle.

4.4.5.4 The Blessing of Jacob: Genesis 49

The tribal list in Jacob's deathbed blessing of his twelve sons has prompted a great deal of discussion because of its supposed value for reconstructing Israel's social, political, and ideological history. The list's supposed antiquity has also spawned an interest in its language and poetic character. Closely related to Gen. 49 are the lists in Deut. 33 (see §9.7) and Judg. 5.

282 H. Seebass. "Die Stämmesprüche Gen 49 3–27." *ZAW* 96 (1984): 333–50.

> The list of tribal sayings in Gen. 49 dates to the pre-monarchic period (ca. twelfth century B.C.E.) and emphasizes the prominence of Joseph. Later redaction during the monarchy (vv. 8b–9) granted prominence to the Davidic tribe of Judah. Although

Simeon appears missing from the list, it is actually represented as "Jeshurun."

283 G. A. Rendsburg. "Israelian Hebrew Features in Genesis 49." *Maarav* 8 (1992): 161–70.

The linguistic features of Gen. 49 suggest that it is a northern composition.

284 R. de Hoop. *Genesis 49 in Its Literary and Historical Context.* OtSt 39. Leiden: Brill, 1999.

The blessings of Gen. 49 must be read within the larger context of Jacob's deathbed scene in Gen. 47:29–49:33. This deathbed tradition originated in the north in the Late Bronze or Early Iron Age and granted prominence to Joseph. This text was later edited in the south during the united monarchy in order to highlight Judah's prominence. The twelve-tribe scheme in Gen. 49 is the product of this Judean redaction.

285 J.-D. Macchi. *Israël et ses tribus selon Genèse 49.* OBO 171. Fribourg: Editions Universitaires; Göttingen: Vandenhoeck & Ruprecht, 1999.

Gen. 49 reflects an old northern six-tribe list subsequently edited to bring the total to twelve tribes. Reuben, Simeon, Levi, and Judah were added during a pro-Judean redaction of the text, while Joseph and Benjamin were added still later, when the south had developed postexilic affections for the north.

286 K. L. Sparks. "Genesis 49 and the Tribal List Tradition in Ancient Israel." *ZAW* 116 (2004): forthcoming.

Gen. 49 is based on an old northern ten-tribe list that granted prominence to Joseph. This list was later revised in the south in order to grant prominence to Judah and to add Simeon and Levi to the list. Judah's claim to prominence was preserved by creating "blessings" that discredited his three older brothers, Reuben, Simeon, and Levi.

5

Prolegomena to Exodus–Deuteronomy

The Books of Exodus, Leviticus, Numbers, and Deuteronomy include a broad range of common themes, traditions, and genres. These include Moses, the wilderness, Hebrew law, covenant ideology, and ritual, among others. For this reason, §§5.1–5.5 provide the bibliographic "prolegomena" for the more detailed bibliographies of each book.

5.1 Moses

Moses is the traditional author of the Pentateuch and stands in the foreground (or looms in the background) on every page of Exodus, Leviticus, Numbers, and Deuteronomy. Although this biblical portrait may reflect historical reminiscences of Israel's great lawgiver, there is an emerging consensus that, in its present form, the Pentateuch presents an elaborated and heroic depiction of Moses. For closely related entries, see especially §6.4.

287 H. Gressman. *Mose und seine Zeit: Ein Kommentar zu den Mose Sagen.* FRLANT 18. Göttingen: Vandenhoeck & Ruprecht, 1913.

> Following the methodological concerns of Gunkel (see #23), seeks to discern the smaller units and traditions behind the Moses tradition in order to distinguish the historic Moses from the heroic and legendary Moses.

288 F. V. Winnett. *The Mosaic Tradition.* Toronto: University of Toronto Press, 1949.

> Reconstructs the primitive Moses tradition through a critical reading of the sources in Exodus, Numbers, and Deuteronomy. Though dated, a very useful discussion.

289 B. S. Childs. "The Birth of Moses." *JBL* 84 (1965): 109–22.

The Moses birth story is an exposure saga that reflects traditions common to the Near East. The story belongs to the latest stages of the exodus tradition's development.

290 D. B. Redford. "The Literary Motif of the Exposed Child." *Numen* 14 (1967): 209–28.

Although the exposure of children is a common motif in folklore and in Near Eastern tradition, the Mesopotamian legend of Sargon's reed-basket exposure is most similar to the birth story of Moses.

291 G. W. Coats. "Legendary Motifs in the Moses Death Reports." *CBQ* 39 (1977): 34–44.

The death reports of Moses present him in idealistic and heroic terms: he retains his physical vitality, his wisdom, and his unusually close relationship with Yahweh. Later reflections on this heroic tradition produced a more realistic and fallible Moses.

292 T. W. Mann. "Theological Reflections on the Denial of Moses." *JBL* 98 (1979): 481–94.

Offers a detailed comparison of the Deuteronomic and Priestly reasons for prohibiting Moses from entering the Promised Land. Deut. 1:34–39 excludes Moses because of Israel's disobedience in the aborted conquest at Kadesh (cf. Num. 13–14), while P (in Deut. 32:48–52) excludes Moses because he did not treat the Lord as holy at Meribah (cf. Num. 20).

293 T. C. Butler. "An Anti-Moses Tradition." *JSOT* 12 (1979): 9–15.

Various texts in the Pentateuch attest to an anti-Moses tradition that reacted against the ideal and legendary depiction of Israel's lawgiver. These texts include Exod. 2:11–25; 4:24–26; 18:1–23; and Num. 12.

294 E. Nielsen. "Moses and the Law." *VT* 32 (1982): 87–98.

Moses was known as Israel's original prophet-leader in the north and was subsequently adopted by northern Deuteronomists as their "law giver." After the fall of the north, Moses was gradually adopted in the south as the exclusive promulgator of all Israelite laws.

295 T. B. Dozeman. "Moses: Divine Servant and Israelite Hero." *HAR* 8 (1984): 45–61.

Moses is portrayed in Exod. 32 as both servant and hero. These roles reflected his dual commitments to Israel and Yahweh, respectively. The text's depiction of Moses borrowed motifs from Near Eastern traditions.

296 G. W. Coats. *Moses: Heroic Man, Man of God.* JSOTSup 57. Sheffield: Sheffield Academic Press, 1988.

Explores the heroic persona of Moses as it emerges in various permutations from the pages of Exodus–Deuteronomy. Moses is both a hero who identifies with his people and a man of God who leads them.

297 S. A. Nigosian. "Moses as They Saw Him." *VT* 43 (1993): 339–50.

The Pentateuch's presentation of Moses is "sacred biography" (as opposed to historical biography), a genre that seeks to express the sacred through the life of an individual who stood in a special relationship to the sacred.

298 J. H. Tigay. "לא נס לחה: 'He Had Not Become Wrinkled' (Deuteronomy 34:7)." Pp. 345–50 in *Solving Riddles and Untying Knots: Biblical, Epigraphic, and Semitic Studies in Honor of Jonas C. Greenfield*. Edited by Z. Zevit et al. Winona Lake, Ind.: Eisenbrauns, 1995.

The root of *ns* is *nss* rather than *nws*. Hence, the reference in Deut. 34:7 should be translated "his [skin's] moisture had not dried up" rather than Moses "had not lost his vigor."

299 R. Rendtorff. "Some Reflections on the Canonical Moses: Moses and Abraham." Pp. 11–19 in *A Biblical Itinerary: In Search of Method, Form, and Content (Essays in Honor of George W. Coats)*. Edited by E. E. Carpenter. JSOTSup 240. Sheffield: Sheffield Academic Press, 1997.

The final form of the Pentateuch explicitly presents Moses as a successor of the patriarchs, especially Abraham.

300 W. H. C. Propp. "Why Moses Could Not Enter the Promised Land." *BRev* 14, no. 3 (1998): 36–40, 42–44.

According to Deuteronomy, Moses was prevented from entering the Promised Land because of the people's sin. P's account in Num. 20, however, lays the blame more specifically on Moses himself. P's pro-Aaron and anti-Moses agenda was likely prompted by competing groups in P's social context, which identified with Aaron and Moses, respectively.

301 E. Otto. "Mose und das Gesetz: Die Mose-Figur als Gegenentwurf politischer Theologie zur neuassyrischen Königsideologie im 7.Jh v. Chr." Pp. 43–83 in *Mose: Agypten und das Alte Testament*. Edited by E. Otto. SBS 189. Stuttgart: BKW, 2000.

During Israel's history, the character Moses was adapted to counter political and theological challenges from Assyria, Babylon, and Persia. The writer of Exodus, for instance, mimicked Sargon's birth story (often considered a neo-Assyrian composition of Sargon II) when he presented Moses' birth. The goal was to contrast the enslaving Assyrian presence with the emancipation provided by the heroic Moses.

5.2 Hebrew Law

Since early in Jewish history, the Pentateuch has been known as a book of law. Although Jewish and Christian traditions have attributed these laws to the great lawgiver, Moses, scholars now suspect that this view is too simple. The laws repeat the same materials at numerous points (a clue that suggests numerous compositions rather than a single composition) and, perhaps more importantly, the laws often treat the same topics from different perspectives. In general, scholars see at least four basic collections of law in the Pentateuch: the Book of the Covenant (BC, in Exod. 20:22–23:33); the Deuteronomic Code (DC, in Deut. 12–26); the Holiness Code (HC, Lev. 17–26); and the Priestly Code (P), which is nested primarily in Leviticus, Numbers, and the second half of Exodus. The nature of each code and the chronological order in which these law collections were composed are now matters of considerable debate. The most common approach among scholars considers the proper order to be BC, DC, HC, and P, but this viewpoint is now increasingly questioned. For additional bibliography, see J. W. Welch, *A Biblical Law Bibliography: Sorted by Subjects and Authors* (Provo, Utah: Brigham Young University, 1989).

5.2.1 Introductory and General Discussions

302 A. Alt. *Die Ursprünge des israelitischen Rechts.* Leipzig: S. Hirzel, 1934. English translation: "The Origins of Israelite Law." Pp. 101–71 in *Essays on Old Testament History and Religion.* Garden City, N.Y.: Doubleday, 1968.

Israelite law reflects both casuistic (if . . . then) and apodictic (thou shalt [not] . . .) forms. The former was borrowed from Canaanite criminal and civil law when Israel entered its land, and the latter reflects Israel's own legal tradition, which emphasizes *lex talionis* (retributive law, i.e., "eye for an eye.").

303 D. Daube. *Studies in Biblical Law.* Cambridge: Cambridge University Press, 1947.

Five classic studies address law in biblical narrative, the use of codas to expand legal codes, the law of retaliation (*lex talionis*), communal responsibility, and *summum ius—summa iniuria* (the problem of law that is too subtle or too scrupulous).

304   R. H. Pfeiffer. *An Introduction to the Old Testament.* Rev.
ed. New York: Harper & Brothers, 1948. [Pp. 210–70.]
A dated but valuable survey of both the primary and secondary
sources relating to the biblical laws. Argues that BC developed
from an original "ritual Decalogue" that is now nested in Exod.
34:10–26. BC was then followed by DC (late seventh century
B.C.E.), HC (sixth century B.C.E.), and P (postexilic).

305   E. Gerstenberger. *Wesen und Herkunft des "apodiktischen
Rechts."* WMANT 20. Neukirchen: Neukirchener Verlag,
1965.
The genre of apodictic law originated in the admonitions of
family wisdom. [For an English introduction to the author's
work, see E. Gerstenberger, "Covenant and Commandment,"
JBL 84 (1965): 38–51.]

306   B. S. Jackson. "The Ceremonial and the Judicial: Biblical
Law as Sign and Symbol." *JSOT* 30 (1984): 25–50.
On the basis of semiotic theory, critiques six common approaches to the study of Hebrew law and then suggests a methodological agenda for the use of semiotics in biblical legal studies.

307   D. Patrick. *Old Testament Law.* Atlanta: John Knox, 1985.
A very useful introduction to Hebrew law. Emphasizes the oral-
ity of the Israelite legal system within which the Pentateuch's
written laws were used.

308   L. M. Bechtel. "Shame as a Sanction of Social Control in
Biblical Israel: Judicial, Political, and Social Shaming."
JSOT 49 (1991): 47–76.
Shame served an important role alongside guilt and punish-
ment in motivating compliance with Israelite law. This strat-
egy works best in group-oriented social structures.

309   M. Fishbane. "Law to Canon: Some 'Ideal-Typical' Stages
of Development." Pp. 65–86 in *Minḥah le-Naḥum: Biblical
and Other Studies Presented to Nahum M. Sarna in Honour of His Seventieth Birthday.* Edited by M. Brettler and
M. Fishbane. JSOTSup 154. Sheffield: Sheffield Academic
Press, 1993.
Suggests a pattern of intracanonical exegesis that led from
Torah instructions, to law code, to the Pentateuch's canonical
combination of law and narrative.

310   B. M. Levinson, ed. *Theory and Method in Biblical and
Cuneiform Law: Revision, Interpolation, and Development.* JSOTSup 181. Sheffield: Sheffield Academic Press,
1994.
This very important collection of essays presents various posi-

tions and perspectives on the composition of biblical and Near Eastern law.

311 G. Brin. *Studies in Biblical Law: From the Hebrew Bible to the Dead Sea Scrolls.* JSOTSup 176. Sheffield: JSOT, 1994.
Isolates patterns of legal growth in Israelite law and then explores these in a detailed study of Hebrew laws of the firstborn.

312 J. Blenkinsopp. *Wisdom and Law in the Old Testament.* 2d ed. Oxford: Oxford University Press, 1995.
Integrates an introduction to Hebrew law with the wisdom traditions from which it sprung.

313 J. Milgrom. "The Truth of Mosaic Origins." Pp. 187–92 in *Mincha: Festgabe für Rolf Rendtorff zum 75. Geburtstag.* Edited by E. Blum. Neukirchen-Vluyn: Neukirchener Verlag, 2000.
The various authors and editors who composed the laws of the Pentateuch viewed their contributions as rooted in Mosaic values. Hence, these legists uniformly credited Moses for their legal compositions.

5.2.2 Near Eastern and Biblical Law

There are many similarities between biblical and Near Eastern laws. Are the biblical laws therefore dependent on Near Eastern law and, if so, in what sense? Some scholars argue that Israel borrowed the laws from the Near East (diffusion), while other scholars argue that similar situations and social predicaments created similar laws (evolutionary models). Still other scholars argue that Israel's laws are actually quite different from their Near Eastern counterparts.

314 M. David. "The Codex Hammurabi and Its Relation to the Provisions of Law in Exodus." Pp. 149–78 in *Oudtestamentische Studiën.* Edited by P. A. H. de Boer. OtSt 7. Leiden: Brill, 1950.
Briefly surveys early responses to the discovery of Hammurabi's laws (HL), which usually assumed that BC's laws were derived from HL. Concludes instead that similarities between the laws are superficial and that the two codes developed independently from each other.

315 S. Paul. *Studies in the Book of the Covenant in the Light of Cuneiform and Biblical Law.* VTSup 17. Leiden: Brill, 1970.
An important comparative study of biblical and Near Eastern laws.

316 R. A. Brauner. "Some Aspects of Offense and Penalty in the

Bible and the Literature of the Ancient Near East." *Gratz College Annual of Jewish Studies* 3 (1974): 9–18.

> In the Near East, laws of retaliation (*lex talionis*) are found in treaties and monumental inscriptions, as well as in laws.

317 N. P. Lemche. "*Andurārum* and *Mīšarum:* Comments on the Problem of Social Edicts and Their Application in the Ancient Near East." *JNES* 38 (1979): 11–22.

> A comparative study of Near Eastern reform edicts (such as the Edict of Ammiṣaduqa) and similar biblical institutions, such as Jubilee and the Sabbath year.

318 T. Frymer-Kensky. "Tit for Tat: The Principle of Equal Retribution in Near Eastern and Biblical Law." *BA* 43 (1980): 230–34.

> *Lex talionis* (retribution law, i.e., "eye for an eye") did not appear in the Bible because of influences from Mesopotamian law. Retributive law originated among Israel's West Semitic forerunners and was then absorbed by the Mesopotamian legal tradition.

319 H. J. Boecker. *Law and the Administration of Justice in the Old Testament and Ancient East.* Minneapolis: Augsburg, 1980.

> Surveys Near Eastern legal codes and jurisprudence, then offers a comparative discussion of the biblical laws.

√ **320** R. Westbrook. *Studies in Biblical and Cuneiform Law.* Paris: J. Gabalda, 1988.

> Ancient Near Eastern legal principles differ from modern law, and the biblical laws reflect this ancient pattern of revenge, ransom, vicarious liability, public authorities' responsibility, pollution, and the extrajudicial role of the king. This Near Eastern pattern is most visible in the oldest code, BC, and is opposed to some extent in DC and P.

321 S. M. Paul. "Biblical Analogues to Middle Assyrian Law." Pp. 333–50 in *Religion and Law: Biblical-Judaic and Islamic Perspectives.* Edited by E. B. Firmage et al. Winona Lake, Ind.: Eisenbrauns, 1990.

> Identifies analogues in Deuteronomy, 2 Isaiah, Ezekiel, and Leviticus.

322 G. J. Wenham. "The Old Testament Attitude to Homosexuality." *Expository Times* 102 (1991): 359–63.

> Although Assyrian and Hittite marriage laws were similar to those in the Hebrew Bible, on the matter of consensual homosexual practices, the Near Eastern laws were generally silent. Scripture's rejection of homosexual behavior is both a deviation and an innovation in comparison with Israel's cultural milieu.

323 G. C. Chirichigno. *Debt-Slavery in Israel and the Ancient Near East.* JSOTSup 141. Sheffield: JSOT, 1993.

Israelite slave laws envision the problem of debt slavery rather than the chattel slavery of Near Eastern law. The differences in the slave laws of Exod. 21, Deut. 15, and Lev. 25 do not stem from a development within Hebrew law but from the fact that the laws deal with somewhat different situations.

324 E. Otto. "Homosexualität im Alten Orient und im Alten Testament." Pp. 322–30 in *Kontinuum und Proprium: Studien zur Sozial-Rechtsgeschichte des Alten Orients und des Alten Testaments.* Orientalia Biblica et Christiana 8. Wiesbaden: Harrassowitz, 1996.

Near Eastern and Old Testament laws concerning homosexuality are similar in terms of what they address (prohibitions of homosexual rape, sex viewed as an act of procreation) and do not address (female homosexuality). However, in contrast to the ambivalence of Near Eastern law, the biblical laws in HC (Lev. 18:22; 20:23) condemn homosexual activity as a violation of divine order and of God's holiness.

325 G. J. Wenham. "The Gap between Law and Ethics in the Bible." *Journal of Jewish Studies* 48 (1997): 17–29.

With regard to avoiding idolatry, homicide, and adultery, the law marked only a minimum standard of behavior. The biblical legists envisioned intimacy with God and love for life as primary motives for obedience.

326 M. Zer-Kavod. "The Code of Hammurabi and the Laws of the Torah." *JBQ* 26 (1998): 107–10.

The striking differences between Hammurabi's laws and the laws of the Pentateuch suggest that the Torah was not dependent on the older Mesopotamian law code.

5.2.3 Composition and Tradition History

327 M. Noth. *Die Gesetze im Pentateuch: Ihre Voraussetzungen und ihr Sinn (Schriften der Königsberger Gelehrten Gesellschaft).* Geisteswissenschaftliche Klasse 17, no. 2. Halle, Germany: Max Niemeyer, 1940. English translation: "The Laws in the Pentateuch: Their Assumptions and Meaning." Pp. 1–105 in *The Laws of the Pentateuch and Other Studies.* Edinburgh and London: Oliver & Boyd, 1966.

The Pentateuchal laws bring together various legal collections from a broad range of specific contexts, ranging from pre-state Israel down to the postexilic period. Apodictic and casuistic forms stand side by side in the Hebrew laws and should not be viewed as sacred and secular, respectively. All of the Hebrew law codes imagine as their proper context the pre-state amphictyony, in which the tribes were unified around a central religious shrine. Hence, the Hebrew legists did not formulate the laws for use in the monarchic legal system but as expressions of ideal law for Israel's ideal political, religious, and social form: the amphictyony.

328 A. Cholewinski. *Heiligkeitsgesetz und Deuteronomium: Eine vergleichende Studie.* AnBib 66. Rome: Biblical Institute Press, 1976.

HC is the product of a rather complex editorial process that attempted to revise the laws of P and especially of DC.

329 E. Otto. "Das Heiligkeitsgesetz Leviticus 17–26 in der Pentateuchredaktion." Pp. 65–80 in *Altes Testament Forschung und Wirkung: Fs H. G. Reventlow.* Frankfurt am Main: Peter Lang, 1994.

The author of HC composed his code after BC, D, and P and, in doing so, managed to link Deuteronomy with the Tetrateuch.

330 I. Knohl. *The Sanctuary of Silence: The Priestly Torah and the Holiness School.* Minneapolis: Fortress, 1995.

HC is an eighth-century composition that mildly corrects the earlier work of P. HC did this in response to the prophetic critique of P's distinction between the cult and morality.

331 C. Carmichael. *The Spirit of Biblical Law.* Athens: University of Georgia Press, 1996.

Third in a trilogy of works arguing that scribes composed Israelite law on the basis of narrative traditions concerning the patriarchs, Moses, the judges, and kings; that is, Hebrew law is a response to Hebrew narrative. This volume focuses on the laws of Leviticus. [See also Carmichael's *Law and Narrative in the Bible* (1985); *The Origins of Biblical Law* (1992); and *Law, Legend, and Incest in the Bible: Leviticus 18–20* (1997). For a critique of Carmichael's approach, see B. M. Levinson, "Calum M. Carmichael's Approach to the Laws of Deuteronomy," *HTR* 83 (1990): 227–57.]

332 F. Crüsemann. *Die Torah: Theologie und Sozialgeschichte des alttestamentlichen Gesetzes.* München: Kaiser, 1992. English translation: *The Torah: Theology and Social History of Old Testament Law.* Minneapolis: Fortress, 1996.

Attempts to reconstruct a history of the origins and development of Israelite law in the context of Israel's social history. BC is the product of a lengthy editorial process and is the oldest code. DC is a response to BC and P (of which HC is a part) is, in turn, a response to DC.

333 E. Otto. *Kontinuum und Proprium: Studien zur Sozial-Rechtsgeschichte des Alten Orients und des Alten Testaments.* Orientalia Biblica et Christiana 8. Wiesbaden: Harrassowitz, 1996.

An important collection of Otto's articles, dating from 1986–96. Five new and eighteen previously published texts. "The Pre-exilic Deuteronomy as a Revision of the Covenant Code," on pp. 112–22, argues that DC is a revision of BC designed to supplement rather than supplant BC.

334 J. Van Seters. "Cultic Laws in the Covenant Code (Exodus 20,22–23,22) and Their Relationship to Deuteronomy and the Holiness Code." Pp. 319–45 in *Studies in the Book of Exodus.* Edited by M. Vervenne. BETL 126. Louvain: Louvain University Press; Peeters, 1996.

A comparative study of BC's laws reveals that it was composed in the exilic period and dates after DC, HC, and the Deuteronomistic History.

335 B. M. Levinson. *Deuteronomy and the Hermeneutics of Legal Innovation.* New York and Oxford: Oxford University Press, 1997.

The authors of Deuteronomy consciously reused and reinterpreted the laws of the Book of the Covenant to promulgate and justify their religious, cultic, and legal reforms. DC is therefore both dependent on, and a radical reformulation of, BC.

336 J. W. Watts. *Reading Law: The Rhetorical Shaping of the Pentateuch.* Biblical Seminar 59. Sheffield: Sheffield Academic Press, 1999.

Repetitions and variations in Hebrew law are usually used to isolate sources and to identify redaction in the laws, but these patterns are better understood as products of a rhetorical strategy that appeals to diverse viewpoints within the author's audience. Like the Greeks and Romans, Hebrew legists improved the rhetorical power of their laws by presenting them in combination with narrative. (In Exod. 19–24 and Deuteronomy, the pattern is stories–lists–sanctions.) This strategy suits well the ancient practice of "publishing" law orally. Although composed of older traditions, the Pentateuchal laws' publication was sponsored by the Persians to secure social stability in Persia's provinces (as was done in Persian Egypt). This final redaction should be associated with P, and its macrostructure was designed to have a persuasive effect on Jews who read or heard the text.

337 J. Van Seters. "Some Observations on the *Lex Talionis* in Exod 21:23–25." Pp. 27–37 in *Recht und Ethos im Alten Testament—Gestalt und Wirkung: Festschrift für Horst Seebass zum 65. Geburtstag.* Edited by S. Beyerle et al. Neukirchen-Vluyn: Neukirchener Verlag, 1999.

BC is an exilic composition that sought to address legal issues presented by two older codes, DC and HC. Strong influences of the Mesopotamian legal tradition on BC support the conclusion that BC was composed during the Babylon exile.

338 E. Otto. "Innerbiblische Exegese im Heiligkeitsgesetz Levitikus 17–26." Pp. 125–96 in *Levitikus als Buch.* Edited by H.-J. Fabry and H.-W. Jüngling. BBB 119. Berlin: Philo, 1999.

HC is a postexilic composition that reformulates legal materials from BC, DC, and P.

5.2.4 Civil and Criminal Law

For a more complete collection of related entries, see also §§6.5.2, 7.7, and 9.5.

339 H. McKeating. "The Development of the Law in Ancient Israel." *VT* 25 (1975): 46–68.

Tests the theory that homicide law evolves from clan law in simple societies (offering redress to the offended kin group) to social and religious laws in complex societies. In Israel, homicide law began in the clan, was modified to serve social purposes during the monarchy, took on both social and sacral dimensions during the late monarchy, and became an entirely sacral offense in postexilic P (because homicide polluted the land).

340 N. P. Lemche. "The 'Hebrew Slave': Comments on the Slave Law (Ex. XXI 2–11)." *VT* 25 (1975): 129–44.

The slave law of Exod. 21:2–16 is based on Near Eastern legal sources and fits into a Canaanite rather than Israelite context. The terms "Hebrew" (*'ibri*) and "free" (*hophshi*) are better translated sociologically, that is, as "outlaw" and "freedman."

341 J. Weingreen. "The Concepts of Retaliation and Compensation in Biblical Law." *Proceedings of the Royal Irish Academy* 76 (1976): 1–11.

Biblical law distinguishes premeditated acts from accidental offenses, with the former treated as criminal acts, requiring retaliation, and the latter as civil acts, requiring compensation.

342 A. G. Auld. "Cities of Refuge in Israelite Tradition." *JSOT* 10 (1978): 26–40.

Examines the relationship between Pentateuchal texts dealing with refuge for the accidental killer and the list of refuge cities in Josh. 20. The list of refuge cities is not a source for the modern historian because it reflects the speculations of an ancient writer.

343 E. W. Davies. "Inheritance Rights and the Hebrew Levirate Marriage, Part 1." *VT* 31 (1981): 138–44; "Inheritance Rights and the Hebrew Levirate Marriage, Part 2." *VT* 31 (1981): 257–68.

Although widows could inherit property in Near Eastern law, this was not the case in Israel. The primary objective of Levirate law was to provide widows with a male heir. The sequel article explores the tendency for potential levirs to reject this responsibility as well as legal efforts to encourage the practice.

344 C. J. H. Wright. "What Happened Every Seven Years in Israel? (Part 1)" *EvQ* 56 (1984): 129–38; "What Happened Every Seven Years in Israel? (Part 2)" *EvQ* 56 (1984): 193–201.

Reconstructs the history and development of Israel's Sabbath-year institution. Part 1 explores fallow land and debt-pledge regulations (arguing that the legal process moved from Exod. 23:10, 11 to Lev. 25:2–7 to Deut. 15:1–3). Part 2 examines the provisions for a seventh-year slave release (Exod. 21:1–6/Deut. 15:12–18) and compares these with Lev. 25:39–43. Humanitarian concerns motivated many of these laws.

345 J. Milgrom. "You Shall Not Boil a Kid in Its Mother's Milk: An Archaeological Myth Destroyed." *BRev* 1 (1985): 48–55.

The thrice-repeated biblical law (Exod. 23:19) that prohibits boiling a kid in its mother's milk cannot be explained by comparison with a supposedly similar Ugaritic text, because that text has been misread. The law's true rationale stems from Israel's dietary system that prohibits the mingling of life and death. It is improper to season a dead animal with what it fed on as a living animal.

346 R. Westbrook. *Property and the Family in Biblical Law.* JSOTSup 113. Sheffield: Sheffield Academic Press, 1991.

A collection of the author's earlier essays that address real-estate transfers, Jubilee, the Levirate law, inheritance, and the function of dowry in marriage law.

347 S. West. "The *Lex Talionis* in the Torah." *JBQ* 21 (1993): 183–88.

Hebrew laws of retribution ("eye for an eye") were not intended for literal implementation but instead expressed a desire for equitable judgment, especially with regard to fair financial compensation.

348   V. H. Matthews, B. M. Levinson, and T. Frymer-Kensky, eds. *Gender and Law in the Hebrew Bible and the Ancient Near East.* JSOTSup 262. Sheffield: Sheffield Academic Press, 1998.

A collection of essays on the role and status of women as reflected in the biblical and Near Eastern law codes.

5.2.5 Religious and Cultic Law

For a more complete collection of related entries, see also §§6.6.1, 7.1–7.8, and 8.5.

349   E. Nielsen. "Some Reflections on the History of the Ark." Pp. 61–74 in *Congress Volume, Oxford, 1959.* VTSup 7. Leiden: Brill, 1960.

Traces the ark's history from the early Israelite traditions down to the postexilic period.

350   G. W. MacRae. "The Meaning and Evolution of the Feast of Tabernacles." *CBQ* 22 (1960): 251–76.

It appears that the Canaanite harvest festival was adopted and transformed into a thanksgiving festival of Yahwism. Also suggests a developmental scheme that explains the sacral calendars of J, E, D, and P, as well as later practices in Judaism.

351   M. Haran. "The Nature of the 'Ohel Mo'edh' in Pentateuchal Sources." *Journal of Semitic Studies* 5 (1960): 50–65.

Early Israelite tradition (JED) represents the ark (*'aron*) and "tent of the meeting" (*'ohel mo'ed*) as separate Priestly and prophetic institutions, respectively. P's concept of a divine dwelling (*mishkan*) combined these institutions, thus transforming the unadorned wooden ark of JED into the golden and ornate throne of Yahweh in P.

352   M. Haran. "The Use of Incense in the Ancient Israelite Ritual." *VT* 10 (1960): 113–29.

There were three uses of incense in ancient Israel: (1) as a supplement to sacrifice; (2) in a censer as an independent sacrifice, offered by an authorized priest within the sanctuary; and (3) on the golden altar as the daily or "perpetual" sacrifice.

353   J. M. Sasson. "Circumcision in the Ancient Near East." *JBL* 85 (1966): 473–76.

Briefly surveys circumcision practices in the Near East and their relationship to the Hebrew practice.

354   H. Gamoran. "The Biblical Law against Loans on Interest." *JNES* 30 (1971): 127–34.

Biblical laws against charging loan interest originated to protect the poor but had the effect of prohibiting even commercial loans to those who were not poor. The extent to which these laws were actually followed is not clear.

355 P. A. H. de Boer. "An Aspect of Sacrifice." Pp. 27–47 in *Studies in the Religion of Ancient Israel.* VTSup 32. Leiden: Brill, 1972.

In antiquity the "bread of presence" (*lehem hapanim*) was stamped with a divine image and, when eaten, nourished the priests for their service to the deity. With respect to the "sweet-smelling aroma" of the sacrifices, it was not the deity who smelled the sacrifice but rather the offerer, who then knew that God had accepted the sacrifice.

356 J. W. McKay. "The Date of Passover and Its Significance." *ZAW* 84 (1972): 435–47.

Attempts to reconstruct the history of the Passover calendar, which by the postexilic period was tied to the newly adopted Babylonian calendar and its solar cycle.

357 N.-E. Andreasen. *The Old Testament Sabbath: A Tradition-Historical Examination.* SBLDS 7. Missoula, Mont.: Society of Biblical Literature, 1972.

An important monographic discussion of Sabbath law and tradition in ancient Israel.

358 M. Haran. "The Passover Sacrifice." Pp. 86–116 in *Studies in the Religion of Ancient Israel.* Edited by G. W. Anderson et al. VTSup 23. Leiden: Brill, 1972.

Wellhausen averred that the Passover was not in E or J and originated as a seventh-century Deuteronomic incarnation of the older practice of sacrificing the firstlings of cattle. It is clear, however, that Passover was known to the older sources (J and E). Moreover, the biblical Passover laws presume in all cases (JEDP) that the practice was undertaken at the temple, so that the "household" format in Exod. 12 was merely an anachronistic attempt to project the temple practice back into the period before the temple or tabernacle existed.

359 D. J. A. Clines. "The Evidence for an Autumnal New Year in Pre-exilic Israel Reconsidered." *JBL* 93 (1974): 22–40.

Although there is no evidence to suggest Israel celebrated an autumnal New Year prior to 605 B.C.E., there is evidence that suggests a spring New Year (the reference to *Abib*, "spring," in the festival "calendars").

360 B. Levine. *In the Presence of the Lord: A Study of Cult and Some Cultic Terms in Ancient Israel.* SJLA 5. Leiden: Brill, 1974.

A detailed discussion of the peace offering (*shelamim*) and the two expiation offerings: the sin offering (hatta't) and the guilt offering ('asham). The terms kipper ("to atone") and zebah ("sacrifice") are also addressed in some detail.

361 J. Milgrom. *Cult and Conscience: The Asham and the Priestly Doctrine of Repentance.* SJLA 18. Leiden: Brill, 1976.

The so-called guilt offering ('asham) was for reparation (and hence included compensation) and differs from the similar hatta't ("sin offering") because 'asham expiates for desecration of the temple sancta while hatta't cleanses the sancta from impurity.

362 D. Davies. "An Interpretation of Sacrifice in Leviticus." *ZAW* 89 (1977): 387–99.

Following W. Robertson Smith, argues that sacrifice both conceives and perpetuates social and religious order.

363 W. W. Hallo. "New Moons and Sabbaths: A Case in the Contrastive Approach." *HUCA* 48 (1977): 1–18.

In contrast to the Mesopotamian lunar calendar and worship of the moon, the Israelite year was based on the week and remained so even after adopting the Babylonian lunar-solar calendar.

✓ **364** M. Haran. *Temples and Temple Service in Ancient Israel.* Oxford: Oxford University Press, 1978.

Reprint

A comprehensive discussion of Israel's ancient rituals and sacrificial cult.

365 J. Milgrom. *Studies in Cultic Theology and Terminology.* SJLA 36. Leiden: Brill, 1983.

An important collection of previous published articles (some originally in Hebrew) that discuss the antiquity of P, the hatta't sacrifice, dietary laws, dedication rites, and other matters ritual and cultic.

366 J. Van Seters. "The Place of the Yahwist in the History of Passover and Massot." *ZAW* 95 (1983): 167–82.

In Exod. 23 and 34, the Yahwist compensated for the absence of sacrifices at Passover during the exile by legislating mas sot (unleavened bread) consumption for seven days instead of one (so the earlier Deuteronomy). During the postexilic period, when sacrifices were restored, D was edited to include both Passover and the seven-day mas sot festival.

367 D. P. Wright. "The Gesture of Hand Placement in the Hebrew Bible and in Hittite Literature." *JAOS* 106 (1986): 433–46.

There are two forms of hand-placement gesture in OT rituals. The two-handed form is used for human beings in nonsacrificial contexts and marks the recipient of ritual action, while the one-handed form designates a sacrificial animal and indicates that the beneficiary of the sacrifice is the one performing the gesture (a similar gesture was used by the Hittites).

368 D. P. Wright. *The Disposal of Impurity in the Priestly Writings of the Bible with Reference to Similar Phenomena in Hittite and Mesopotamian Cultures.* SBLDS 101. Atlanta: Scholars, 1987.

A comparative study of Hebrew and Near Eastern rites for disposing of ritual pollution. Especially relevant to interpreting the atonement ritual in Lev. 16.

369 G. Robinson. *The Origin and Development of the Old Testament Sabbath: A Comprehensive Exegetical Approach.* BBET 21. Frankfurt am Main: Lang, 1988.

An important monographic discussion of Sabbath law and tradition in ancient Israel.

370 N. Zohar. "Repentance and Purification: The Significance and Semantics of חטאת in the Pentateuch." *JBL* 107 (1988): 609–18.

In the Israelite sin offering, contamination was transferred from sinner, to animal, to blood, and then to the sanctuary, where God's power contained it (or destroyed it?) until the annual purgation on the Day of Atonement.

371 B. R. Goldstein and A. M. Cooper. "The Festivals of Israel and Judah and the Literary History of the Pentateuch." *JAOS* 110 (1990): 19–31.

Israel's sacred feasts reflect the conflation of several different festival calendars. Fortunately, the northern and southern festival calendars can be reconstructed, as can the process by which they were combined.

372 J. Milgrom. "Ethics and Ritual: The Foundations of Biblical Dietary Laws." Pp. 159–91 in *Religion and Law: Biblical-Judaic and Islamic Perspectives.* Edited by E. B. Firmage et al. Winona Lake, Ind.: Eisenbrauns, 1990.

The criteria used in biblical dietary laws were developed on the basis of animals already normally consumed (e.g., livestock) and were gradually expanded to exclude animals that were not eaten. The dietary laws taught Israel a reverence for life by reducing the choice of flesh that Israel could consume, prescribing humane methods for slaughter, and prohibiting the ingestion of blood out of respect for life. Adherence to this pattern therefore reflected ethical holiness.

373 D. P. Wright. "The Spectrum of Priestly Impurity." Pp.

150–81 in *Priesthood and Cult in Ancient Israel.* Edited by
G. A. Anderson and S. M. Olyan. JSOTSup 125. Sheffield:
JSOT, 1991.

> The Priestly rationale for classifying different sorts of impurity
> reflects a scaled spectrum but distinguishes between "toler-
> ated" pollution and prohibited pollution (although at the mar-
> gins of the spectrum, the difference between them is quite
> thin).

374 J. Milgrom. "The Priestly Laws of Sancta Contamination."
Pp. 137–46 in *"Sha'arei Talmon": Studies in the Bible,
Qumran, and the Ancient Near East Presented to She-
maryahu Talmon.* Edited by M. Fishbane and E. Tov. Winona Lake, Ind.: Eisenbrauns, 1992.

> Among other things, concludes that contamination of the Isra-
> elite sanctuary varied directly with both the intensity of the
> impurity source and the intensity of the sanctuary's purity; it
> varied inversely with distance. Contamination also had a min-
> imum threshold, below which it effected no contamination of
> the sanctuary.

375 C. J. Labuschagne. "'You Shall Not Boil a Kid in Its
Mother's Milk': A New Proposal for the Origin of the Pro-
hibition." Pp. 6–17 in *The Scriptures and the Scrolls: Fs
A. S. van der Woude.* Edited by A. de Groot and D. T. Ariel.
Qedem 33. Jerusalem: Institute of Archaeology, Hebrew
University, 1992.

> Labuschagne surveys the many attempts to explain this prohi-
> bition and then offers his own solution: the text forbids boiling
> the kid in its mother's colostrum because the colostrum con-
> tains blood, and the eating of blood is prohibited.

376 W. Houston. *Purity and Monotheism: Clean and Unclean
Animals in Biblical Law.* JSOTSup 140. Sheffield: JSOT,
1993.

> The classifications of clean and unclean animals in Lev. 11 and
> Deut. 14 both originated in Priestly circles. Generally, the
> taboos do not follow from the criteria so much as the criteria
> were developed to reflect the taboos.

377 M. Weinfeld. "The Ban on the Canaanites in Biblical Codes
and Its Historical Development." Pp. 142–60 in *History
and Tradition of Early Israel: Studies Presented to Eduard
Nielsen.* Edited by A. Lemaire and B. Otzen. VTSup 50. Leiden: Brill, 1993.

> Early Hebrew law prescribed expelling Canaanites and pro-
> scribed covenants with them (Exod. 23:20–33; 34:11–16). The

next stage of development (P) prescribed dispossessing the Canaanites (Num. 33:50–56). The so-called ban (*herem*), found in Deut. 7:2 and 20:16–17, represented the final stage in the development of these laws. Although it prescribed the total military destruction of Canaanites, this was merely a utopian vision and was never implemented.

378 R. T. Beckwith and M. J. Selman. *Sacrifice in the Bible.* Grand Rapids: Baker; Carlisle, England: Paternoster, 1995.

Includes essays on "The Passover Sacrifice" (T. D. Alexander); "The Levitical Sacrificial System" (P. P. Jenson); "Sacrifice in the Ancient Near East" (M. J. Selman); and "The Theology of Old Testament Sacrifice" (G. J. Wenham).

379 D. Patrick. "The First Commandment in the Structure of the Pentateuch." *VT* 45 (1995): 107–18.

The Pentateuch holds human beings responsible only for what they explicitly know. For this reason, polemic against idolatry is introduced only after the first commandment of the Decalogue (contra idolatry) was given.

380 S. M. Olyan. "Why an Altar of Unfinished Stones? Some Thoughts on Ex 20,25 and Dtn 27,5–6." *ZAW* 108 (1996): 161–71.

Some Israelite laws prescribe the use of unhewn stones in altars as an expression of wholeness and completeness in worship.

381 A. M. Cooper and B. R. Goldstein. "At the Entrance to the Tent: More Cultic Resonances in Biblical Narrative." *JBL* 116 (1997): 201–15.

Proposes a four-stage tradition history for God's tent-dwelling in the Hebrew Bible: (1) pre-literary stage; (2) first literary stage by redactor who composed J and E ("tent of the assembly"/ *'ohel mo'ed*); (3) P's tent in the *miškan*; and (4) the holiness school's distinctive *'ohel mo'ed* in Num. 27. This tradition history was shaped by variations in intermediation and power in ancient Israel.

382 K. L. Sparks. "A Comparative Study of the Biblical נבלה Laws." *ZAW* 110 (1998): 594–600.

A comparison of the biblical laws that address the *nevelah* ("a [clean] animal that dies of itself") and the *terefah* ("a [clean] animal killed by a unclean carnivore") suggests that the proper chronological relationship of the laws is D, HC, BC, then P.

383 D. Fleming. "The Biblical Tradition of Anointing Priests." *JBL* 117 (1998): 401–14.

The Priestly anointing tradition did not originate during the exile, as some scholars assert, but was instead a practice long known in the ancient Near East. Although different, the anointing traditions in Exod. 28 and Lev. 8 do not reflect a diachronic pattern of development but instead are complementary.

384   G. Braulik. "Were Women, Too, Allowed to Offer Sacrifices in Israel? Observations on the Meaning and Festive Form of Sacrifice in Deuteronomy." *Hervormde Teologiese Studies* 55 (1999): 909–42.

Although sacrifices in ancient Israel were normally performed by the male head of the household, Deuteronomy permitted women to offer sacrifices if the head of household was unable to do so. P seems to have followed this precedent.

385   D. E. Fleming. "The Israelite Festival Calendar and Emar's Ritual Archive." *RB* 106 (1999): 8–34.

The Priestly festival calendar of Israel is comparable to the ritual calendar of Emar. This suggests that the ritual calendar of Israel should be understood to reflect the broader ritual context of the ancient Near East.

386   P. Heger. *The Three Biblical Altar Laws.* BZAW 279. Berlin: de Gruyter, 1999.

Traces the history of sacrificial law from early Israel down to the replacement of sacrifice by the synagogue. Special attention is given to the relationship between the altar laws in Exod. 20:21–23; 27:1–8; and Deut. 27:5–6.

387   J. Goldingay. "The Significance of Circumcision." *JSOT* 88 (2000): 3–18.

Circumcision is by its nature a gender-exclusive covenant sign. Narratives whose theme is circumcision highlight the special responsibilities associated with male sexuality and focus, more generally, on the inner spiritual qualities that are important for religious faith.

5.2.6 The Decalogue

Three versions of the Decalogue appear in the Hebrew Bible (Exod. 20; Exod. 34; and Deut. 5). The versions in Exod. 20 and Deut. 5 are virtually identical but offer differing motivations for keeping the Sabbath. Exod. 34 is a different matter that is addressed in §11.6.2. The two primary interpretive and historical issues are (1) Which is the older Decalogue, Exod. 20 or Deut. 5? and (2) Is the Decalogue an ancient foundation for Israelite law or a late attempt to summarize the principles of Hebrew law?

388   E. Nielsen. *Die Zehn Gebote: Eine traditionsgeschicht-*

liche Skizze. Copenhagen: Prostant Apud Munksgaard, 1965. English translation: *The Ten Commandments in New Perspective.* SBT, 2d ser. London: SCM Press, 1968.

The Decalogue (Exod. 20; Deut. 5) was composed in the north as a basic standard of behavior. Portions of this tradition go back to Moses, but certainly not the Decalogue itself. Various expansions, abbreviations, and other changes have altered the text's original form.

389 J. J. Stamm and M. E. Andrew. *The Ten Commandments in Recent Research.* SBT, 2d ser. London: SCM Press, 1967.

An extensive survey of then-recent scholarship, followed by a brief but detailed exegetical discussion of the Decalogue.

390 B. Lang. "Neues über den Dekalog." *Theologische Quartalschrift* 164 (1984): 58–65.

The exilic version of the Decalogue in Deut. 5 is older than the version found in Exod. 20.

391 M. Weinfeld. "The Decalogue: Its Significance, Uniqueness, and Place in Israel's Tradition." Pp. 3–47 in *Religion and Law: Biblical-Judaic and Islamic Perspectives.* Edited by E. B. Firmage et al. Winona Lake, Ind.: Eisenbrauns, 1990.

"At the dawn of Israelite history the Decalogue was promulgated [under Moses] . . . as the foundation document of the Israelite community, written on two stone tablets" (32). This summary of basic covenant obligations was recited during the annual Feast of Weeks celebration, as is reflected in Ps. 50 and 81.

392 R. Youngblood. "Counting the Ten Commandments." *BRev* 10, no. 6 (1994): 30–35, 50, 52.

The two tablets of Moses were vassal and suzerain copies, respectively, such as we see in Hittite treaties of the second millennium B.C.E. [Cf. the similar thesis of J. Derby, "The Two Tablets of the Covenant," *JBQ* 21 (1993): 73–79.]

393 R. G. Kratz. "Der Dekalog im Exodusbuch." *VT* 44 (1994): 205–38.

The Decalogue (Exod. 20:1–17) was composed as a summary of, and introduction to, BC. The Decalogue of Deut. 5 is later than and dependent on the version in Exodus.

394 R. E. Tappy. "The Code of Kinship in the Ten Commandments." *RB* 107 (2000): 321–37.

The second half of the Ten Commandments (Exod. 20; Deut. 5) stems from an old tradition designed to promote solidarity within Israelite households. This original function was lost when the tradition was adopted as a preamble in the Israelite legal collections.

5.2.7 Motive Clauses in Biblical Law

After Deuteronomy forbids charging interest to a fellow Hebrew in 23:19–20, the law goes on to say, "in order that the LORD
your God may bless you in all that you undertake in the land
which you are entering to take possession of it." This last phrase
is called a motive clause because it provides a motivation or reason for following the legal prescription. These clauses are particularly prominent in Deuteronomy and the Holiness Code but appear in other biblical codes as well. Studies of these clauses have
generally focused on two issues: (1) form and function; and
(2) whether the motive clauses originated with the laws or were
added to them later.

395 B. Gemser. "The Importance of the Motive Clause in Old
Testament Law." Pp. 50–66 in *Congress Volume, Copenhagen, 1953.* VTSup 1. Leiden: Brill, 1953.

Motive clauses do not appear in Near Eastern laws, and in the
case of Hebrew law there are fewer in early law codes than in
later codes. The motive clauses were not added to the laws
later, as some suppose, but are integral to the laws.

396 R. Sonsino. *Motive Clauses in Hebrew Law: Biblical
Forms and Near Eastern Parallels.* SBLDS 45. Chico,
Calif.: Scholars Press, 1980.

Hebrew law appeals to four basic motives in these clauses:
God's authority, historical experience, fear of punishment, and
promise of blessing. While Near Eastern law also includes motive clauses, the Hebrew law differs because the clauses are
more common and because Hebrew motive clauses have been
influenced by the wisdom tradition.

397 P. Doron. "Motive Clauses in the Laws of Deuteronomy:
Their Forms, Functions, and Contents." *HAR* 2 (1989):
61–77.

Motive clauses occur in seven basic forms in Deuteronomy.
Functionally speaking, these fall out into four basic categories:
(1) motivation by appeal to the value of human life and dignity;
(2) motivation by emphasizing Israel's special status; (3) motivation by promise of reward; and (4) didactic motivations.

5.3 Treaty and Covenant in the Pentateuch

The covenant themes in the Pentateuch reflect traits and
patterns that also appear in ancient Near Eastern treaty texts. As
a result, scholars have attempted to date the biblical covenant

texts by comparing them to Near Eastern treaties. Older scholarship often accentuated the similarities between the Pentateuchal covenants and Hittite treaties, but it is now more common to stress the influence of later treaties, especially the neo-Assyrian texts. This last approach often views Israel's covenant ideology as a polemic against neo-Assyrian imperialism (eighth to seventh centuries B.C.E.). Two other tendencies are also visible in contemporary biblical study of covenant ideology: (1) there is a strong propensity to see the emergence of covenantal ideology as a very late development in Israelite history; and (2) in a related matter, the Sinai covenantal tradition, which was previously viewed as very ancient, is now increasingly viewed as a latecomer to Israelite tradition. For important related entries, see §§5.2, 6.5, and chapter 9.

398 G. E. Mendenhall. "Ancient Oriental and Biblical Law." *BA* 17 (1954): 26–46; "Covenant Forms in Israelite Tradition." *BA* 17 (1954): 50–76.

> The covenant traditions in Deuteronomy, the Decalogue, and the Sinai pericope (Exod. 19–24) are similar to second-millennium Hittite treaties and therefore reflect a very ancient covenant tradition.

399 D. J. McCarthy. *Treaty and Covenant.* AnBib 21. Rome: Pontifical Biblical Institute, 1963. Second edition: AnBib 21a. Rome: Pontifical Biblical Institute, 1978.

> The oldest forms of the Decalogue and Sinai tradition do not reflect ancient treaty forms. A treaty form similar to that found in the second-millennium Hittite treaties, however, was later applied to these traditions. In the case of Deuteronomy, its similarities to Hittite treaties cannot be used to date the book to the second millennium because Deuteronomy also shares many features with first-millennium Assyrian treaties.

400 M. Kline. *Treaty of the Great King.* Grand Rapids: Eerdmans, 1963.

> Similarities between Deuteronomy and ancient Hittite treaties support the dating of the Pentateuch to the second millennium B.C.E.

401 R. Frankena. "The Vassal-Treaties of Esarhaddon and the Dating of Deuteronomy." Pp. 122–54 in כה: *1940–1965, Oudtestamentlich Werkgezelschap in Nederland.* OtSt 14. Leiden: Brill, 1965.

> The close similarities between Deuteronomy and Esarhaddon's seventh-century neo-Assyrian vassal treaties indeed support

the usual dating of Deuteronomy to the seventh century B.C.E. Deuteronomy's treaty form was an act of resistance against Assyrian domination.

402 M. Weinfeld. "Traces of Assyrian Treaty Formulae in Deuteronomy." *Biblica* 46 (1965): 417–27.
> Points out features that Deuteronomy shares with first-millennium neo-Assyrian treaties.

403 D. J. McCarthy. *Old Testament Covenant: A Survey of Current Opinions.* Atlanta: John Knox, 1972.
> A dated but valuable survey of covenant and treaty scholarship as it regards the biblical traditions.

404 L. Perlitt. *Bundestheologie im Alten Testament.* WMANT 36. Neukirchen-Vluyn: Neukirchener Verlag, 1969.
> Israel's concept of a religious convent with Yahweh and the expression of this relationship in a treaty/covenant form did not develop much earlier than the seventh century B.C.E. [This view is now common among scholars.]

405 E. W. Nicholson. *Exodus and Sinai in History and Tradition.* Richmond: John Knox, 1973.
> The oldest level of the ancient Sinai tradition (Exod. 24:9–11) includes the theophany and a sacred meal, but no covenant, no Moses, and no exodus. This leaves open the possibility that the covenant concept developed very late in Israel's history.

406 T. E. McComiskey. *The Covenants of Promise: A Theology of the Old Testament Covenants.* Grand Rapids: Baker, 1985.
> An important evangelical discussion of the covenant theme as it originated in the Pentateuch and as it was subsequently developed in the biblical traditions.

407 E. W. Nicholson. "Covenant in a Century of Study since Wellhausen." Pp. 54–69 in *Prophets, Worship, and Theodicy: Studies in Prophetism, Biblical Theology, and Structural and Rhetorical Analysis and on the Place of Music in Worship.* OtSt 24. Leiden: Brill, 1986.
> Surveys modern study of Israel's covenant ideology since Wellhausen.

408 E. W. Nicholson. *God and His People: Covenant and Theology in the Old Testament.* Oxford: Clarendon, 1986.
> Criticizes Perlitt's thesis (#404) that Israel's covenant ideology emerged only in the seventh century B.C.E. and adduces evidence that the covenant concept is older.

409 D. R. Hillers. "*Rite:* Ceremonies of Law and Treaty in the Ancient Near East." Pp. 351–64 in *Religion and Law: Bib-*

lical-Judaic and Islamic Perspectives. Edited by E. B. Firmage et al. Winona Lake, Ind.: Eisenbrauns, 1990.

Discusses the importance of ratification ceremonies in ancient treaties.

410 G. E. Mendenhall. "The Suzerainty Treaty Structure: Thirty Years Later." Pp. 85–100 in *Religion and Law: Biblical-Judaic and Islamic Perspectives.* Edited by E. B. Firmage et al. Winona Lake, Ind.: Eisenbrauns, 1990.

Explores the political, ideological, and religious implications that Israel's adoption of the treaty form has, or should have, for modern society.

5.4 The History and Development of Israel's Priesthood

Scholars have long noted that there is a discernible pattern of development in Israel's priesthood. According to Wellhausen (#22), this development included five stages: (1) an early period with no fixed priesthood but an emerging guild of Levitical priests (see Judges, Samuel); (2) the development of two competing priestly guilds during the early monarchy, the Levites and Zadokites (the Zadokites became more prominent and powerful [see Samuel–Kings]); (3) a late-monarchic attempt to restore the fortunes of the Levitical priesthood by granting it equal status with the Zadokites (see Deuteronomy); (4) the exilic promotion of the Zadokites as the sole priests and the demotion of the Levites to a status as temple servants (Ezekiel); and (5) the further legitimation of the Zadokite grip on the priesthood during the postexilic period, when P traced its origins to an ancient priestly forefather, Aaron (Ezekiel, P, Ezra, Nehemiah, Chronicles). Some scholars have taken issue with Wellhausen's views while others have refined them.

411 G. E. Wright. "The Levites in Deuteronomy." *VT* 4 (1954): 325–30.

Deuteronomy distinguishes between Levitical priests, who serve as altar clergy, and client Levites, who serve no altar functions.

412 J. A. Emerton. "Priests and Levites in Deuteronomy: An Examination of Dr. G. E. Wright's Theory." *VT* 12 (1962): 129–38.

Finds wanting Wright's thesis (cf. #411) that in Deuteronomy, as in P, priests and Levites are distinguished. Deuteronomy clearly views all Levites as qualified to serve at the altar, while this is certainly not true of P.

413 A. Cody. *A History of the Old Testament Priesthood.*
AnBib 35. Rome: Pontifical Biblical institute, 1969.
Offers this historical reconstruction of Israelite priesthood:
(1) Levi was originally a secular tribe; (2) the Priestly sons of Eli
were Levities, and David's priest Abiathar was their heir;
(3) under Solomon, the Levitical Abiathar was replaced by the
non-Levitical Zadok; (4) in Deuteronomy (late monarchy) the
Levites continued their struggle against the Zadokites for recognition; (5) during the exile, the Levitical Kohathites succeeded
in gaining Priestly recognition, reinforcing this position by con-
verting Aaron, Israel's ancient *non-Priestly* leader, into their
Priestly forefather (hence, both Aaronids and Zadokites made
successful claims to the priesthood; these two groups assimi-
lated into one, leaving the other Levites to work as temple servants); and (6) when the Jews returned from the exile, the high
priest's authority emerged in the absence of a national kingdom.

414 F. M. Cross. "The Priestly Houses of Early Israel." Pp. 195–
215 in *Canaanite Myth and Hebrew Epic.* Cambridge: Harvard University Press, 1973.
Attempts to reconstruct the history of Israel's priesthood on
the basis of Priestly genealogies and the Pentateuchal conflict
stories (Exod. 32; Lev. 10; Num. 12; 16–17; 25).

415 M. A. Cohen. "The Role of the Shilonite Priesthood in the
United Monarchy of Ancient Israel." *HUCA* 36 (1965):
59–98.

416 R. Abba. "Priests and Levites in Deuteronomy." *VT* 27
(1977): 257–67.
Questions Wellhausen's equation that "Levite" equals "priest" in
Deuteronomy and concludes that P's distinction between priests
and Levites originated before the exile and is reflected in D.

417 M. White. "The Elohistic Depiction of Aaron: A Study in
the Levite-Zadokite Controversy." Pp. 149–59 in *Studies
in the Pentateuch.* Edited by J. A. Emerton. VTSup 41. Leiden: E. J. Brill, 1990.
E, the national court historian of Jeroboam in the north, took
up older traditions about Israel's apostasy (Exod. 32) and Miriam's rebellion (Num. 12) and turned these into critiques of
Aaron and the non-Levitical Zadokite priesthood in Jerusalem.
E did this to uphold the authority and rights of the Levitical
priests who worked in the north in Bethel.

5.5 The Wilderness Tradition

In the Hebrew Prophets, Israel's "wilderness" experience is
sometimes recalled with pleasant nostalgia (e.g., Hos. 2:14–15

[2:16–17 in Hebrew]) and at other points with disdain (e.g., Ezek. 20:13). This has prompted scholars to look closely at the wilderness traditions in the Pentateuch, which tend to present a positive viewpoint before Sinai (in Exodus) and a decisively negative viewpoint after Sinai (in Numbers). The usual presumption nowadays is that the wilderness story originated as a tradition about Israel's positive experiences with Yahweh and that this was later transformed into a negative tradition, but this remains a matter of debate.

418 G. W. Coats. *Rebellion in the Wilderness: The Murmuring Motif in the Wilderness Traditions of the Old Testament.* Nashville and New York: Abingdon, 1968.

> Although the primitive wilderness tradition affirmed Yahweh's provision for Israel and Israel's faithful response to its God, J added the motif of wilderness rebellion as a Judean polemic against the northern cult. His purpose was to show that Israel's forefathers had forfeited their divine election, which now belonged to the Davidic monarchy.

419 S. J. de Vries. "The Origin of the Murmuring Tradition." *JBL* 87 (1968): 51–58.

> J's original murmuring tradition does not reflect Israel's rebellion.

420 G. W. Coats. "The Wilderness Itinerary." *CBQ* 34 (1972): 135–52.

> Although three separate traditions may lie behind the wilderness itinerary (exodus, conquest, Sinai), in their present context these elements have been combined into a single whole.

421 G. I. Davies. *The Way of the Wilderness.* Society of Old Testament Studies Monograph Series 5. New York: Cambridge University Press, 1979.

> A detailed geographical study of the wilderness itinerary of the Pentateuch.

422 R. J. Burns. *Has the Lord Indeed Spoken Only through Moses? A Study of the Biblical Portrait of Miriam.* SBLDS 84. Atlanta: Scholars, 1987.

> The biblical tradition remembers Miriam as a cultic leader with authority similar to that of Aaron and Moses. Her squabbles with Moses reflect a conflict about oracular authority rather than domestic concerns.

423 G. I. Davies. "The Wilderness Itineraries and Recent Archaeological Research." Pp. 161–75 in *Studies in the Pentateuch.* Edited by J. A. Emerton. VTSup 41. Leiden: E. J. Brill, 1990.

> Critiques recent attempts to correlate the wilderness itineraries of Numbers with archaeological data.

424   M. S. Smith. "Matters of Space and Time in Exodus and Numbers." Pp. 182–207 in *Theological Exegesis: Essays in Honor of Brevard S. Childs.* Edited by C. Seitz and K. E. Greene-McCreight. Grand Rapids: Eerdmans, 1999.

Chronologically, thematically, and geographically, the wilderness traditions in Exodus and Numbers form a symmetrical structure around the Sinai material in Exod. 19–Num. 10. This structure highlights the contrast between a positive tone in the wilderness of Exodus and the sin and rebellion in the wilderness of Numbers.

6

Exodus

The exodus story is foundational for Jewish theology and is also important in Christian tradition. This story is nested in a book filled with narrative intrigue, interpretive conundrums, and a breadth of subject matter that includes narrative, law, ritual prescription, and divine theophany. From a modern perspective, the book also confronts us with numerous historical issues and problems.

6.1 General Discussions

425 A. M. Cooper and B. R. Goldstein. "Exodus and *Maṣṣôt* in History and Tradition." *Maarav* 8 (1992): 15–37.
   The exodus is a northern tradition that accounts for Israel's origins. The northern festival of unleavened bread (*maṣṣôt*) was at some point combined with the exodus tradition.

426 M. Vervenne, ed. *Studies in the Book of Exodus.* BETL 126. Louvain: Louvain University Press; Peeters, 1996.
   An important collection of contemporary essays on the Book of Exodus.

427 G. I. Davies. "The Theology of Exodus." Pp. 137–52 in *In Search of True Wisdom: Essays in Old Testament Interpretation in Honour of Ronald E. Clements.* Edited by E. Ball. JSOTSup 300. Sheffield: Sheffield Academic Press, 1999.
   Law, salvation, and covenant are commonly suggested as the central theological themes of Exodus. Davies suggests that a more appropriate theme is divine presence because it can include all of these earlier suggestions while accounting, at the same time, for other materials in the book.

6.2 Composition, Authorship, Context

These entries supplement those found in chapter 3.

428 S. McEvenue. "The Speaker(s) in Ex 1–15." Pp. 220–36 in
*Biblische Theologie und gesellschaftlicher Wandel: Für
Norbert Lohfink, SJ.* Edited by G. Braulik. Freiburg: Herder,
1993.
> Contra E. Blum, argues that Exod. 1–15 was compiled by an ed-
> itor who made little effort to alter his sources for the sake of
> coherence.

429 J. Blenkinsopp. "Structure and Meaning in the Sinai-Horeb
Narrative (Exodus 19–34)." Pp. 109–25 in *A Biblical Itin-
erary: In Search of Method, Form, and Content (Essays in
Honor of George W. Coats).* Edited by E. E. Carpenter.
JSOTSup 240. Sheffield: Sheffield Academic Press, 1997.
> The Sinai-Horeb narrative in Exod. 19–34 was inserted by a
> Deuteronomic author to emphasize moral obligation and the
> need for divine assistance in a new covenant, in which Yahweh
> circumcises the heart of Israel.

6.3 The Exodus in History and Tradition

There is an ongoing debate among scholars concerning the
historicity of the exodus tradition. To what extent is the exodus
a literary tradition as opposed to an account of actual events?
The present trend is toward literary readings and away from
rigidly historical readings of the exodus. Many scholars stand between these two extremes, admitting that there may be some
kernel of historicity in the story but concluding that it is impossible to reconstruct this historical sequence because of the literary character of the sources.

430 J. Bimson. *Redating the Exodus and Conquest.* JSOTSup 5.
Sheffield: JSOT, 1978.
> Archaeological and historical data suggest that the fifteenth
> century b.c.e. provides a better context for the exodus than
> does the commonly held thirteenth-century view.

431 G. B. Geyer. "The Joseph and Moses Narratives: Folk-Tale
and History." *JSOT* 15 (1980): 51–56.
> Critiques recent attempts by T. L. Thompson and D. Irvin to
> discard the historical content of the Joseph and Moses narra-
> tives because they are similar to Near Eastern folktales.

432 W. Johnstone. "The Exodus as Process." *Expository Times*
91 (1980): 358–63.

The exodus narrative is a simplified theological interpretation of the past rather than a strictly historical composition.

433 B. Halpern. "Radical Exodus Redating Fatally Flawed." *BAR* 13, no. 6 (1987): 56–61.

Recent attempts to date the exodus early (to the fifteenth century B.C.E.; see Bimson [#430]) are fraught with textual, historical, and archaeological problems.

434 A. Perevolotsky and I. Finkelstein. "The Southern Sinai Exodus Route in Ecological Perspective." *BAR* 11, no. 4 (1985): 26–41.

The association of biblical sites of the exodus itinerary with modern locations stems from contemporary ecological considerations rather than from ancient historical fact.

435 D. B. Redford. "An Egyptological Perspective on the Exodus Narrative." Pp. 137–61 in *Egypt, Israel, Sinai: Archaeological and Historical Relationships in the Biblical Period*. Edited by A. F. Rainey. Tel Aviv: Tel Aviv University, 1987.

When the biblical account of Israel's bondage and exodus is compared with Egyptian evidence, the results suggest that the Book of Exodus contains little if any historical, literary, or folkloristic material of Egyptian origin.

436 L. B. Couroyer. "L'Exode et la bataille de Qadesh." *RB* 97 (1990): 321–58.

Correspondence between the biblical account of the exodus and the Egyptian Qadesh battle reliefs supports the conclusion that these inscriptions inspired portions of the exodus tradition itself (e.g., Hittite charioteers perishing in the sea).

437 B. Halpern. "The Exodus from Egypt: Myth and Reality." Pp. 86–117 in *The Rise of Ancient Israel*. Edited by H. Shanks. Washington, D.C.: Biblical Archaeology Society, 1992.

The exodus and the closely related Joseph story reflect distorted memories of the Hyksos expulsion from Egypt and of the Asiatic outlaws called the *Hapiru*.

438 C. R. Krahmalkov. "Exodus Itinerary Confirmed by the Evidence." *BAR* 20 (1994): 54–62, 79.

External evidence suggest that the Israelite Exodus itinerary as reflected in the Hebrew Bible is historically accurate.

439 E. S. Frerichs and L. H. Lesko, eds. *Exodus: The Egyptian Evidence*. Winona Lake, Ind.: Eisenbrauns, 1997.

A collection of essays that conclude there is very little evidence for the historicity of the Israelite exodus from Egypt.

440 J. K. Hoffmeier. *Israel in Egypt: The Evidence for the Au-*

thenticity of the Exodus Tradition. New York and Oxford: Oxford University Press, 1997.

> Examines the Egyptian evidence and concludes that the Hebrew narratives about Joseph and the exodus are historically accurate. Admits, however, "the absence of direct archaeological or historical evidence" (x).

441 A. Millard. "How Reliable Is Exodus?" *BAR* 26, no. 4 (2000): 50–57.

> The details of the exodus tradition satisfactorily fit into what is known about Late Bronze Age Egypt. There is no reason to presuppose that the exodus is merely a fiction.

442 R. S. Hendel. "The Exodus in Biblical Memory." *JBL* 120 (2001): 601–22.

> The themes and motifs of the Exodus story reflect history in three scales: events (historical happenings), conjunctures (models and traditions of social identity), and *longue durée* (the Exodus story as it resonates over time). While there are actual historical elements behind the exodus tradition (e.g., epidemics in Egypt, slaves in Egypt, the figure of Moses), these have been obscured by their transposition into the larger scales of history.

6.4 From Slavery to Sinai: Interpreting Exodus 1–18

Exod. 1–18 addresses the origins of the Israelite enslavement, the emergence of Mosaic leadership, the plagues, and the divine deliverance and subsequent trek of Israel to Sinai. For related entries, see §§5.1 and 5.5.

443 M. Greenberg. *Understanding Exodus.* Heritage of Biblical Israel, 2d ser. New York: Behrman House for the Melton Research Center of the Jewish Theological Seminary of America, 1969.

> This classic interpretation and discussion of Exod. 1–12 gives attention to both synchronic and diachronic dimensions of the text.

444 Z. Zevit. "The Priestly Redaction and the Interpretation of the Plague Narrative in Exodus." *JQR* 66 (1966): 193–211.

> Concludes that Priestly redactor portrayed Egypt as a land without people, animals, or vegetation, that is, as a land in which the creation of Gen. 1–2 was "undone."

445 G. W. Coats. "Moses in Midian." *JBL* 92 (1973): 3–10.

> The kernel of the tradition about Moses in Midian (Exod. 3:1–4:18) lies in the marriage story. However, the purpose of the narrative is to connect Moses with his Midianite father-in-law, not his wife.

446 M. Gilula. "The Smiting of the First-Born—An Egyptian Myth?" *Tel Aviv* 4 (1977): 94–95.

Pyramid and coffin texts suggest an ancient Egyptian tradition in which the firstborn of gods, men, and animals were killed in a single event. This tradition may lie behind the biblical Passover tradition.

447 R. R. Wilson. "The Hardening of Pharaoh's Heart." *CBQ* 41 (1979): 18–36.

The hardening motif did not originate as a literary device to connect disparate plague stories, but it does serve an integrative literary and theological role in Exod. 4–14. While Pharaoh hardens his own heart in J, in E, and even more in P, it is the sovereign God of Israel who hardens the king's heart. Israel is thereby warned to avoid the folly of refusing to listen to Yahweh.

448 J. Van Seters. "The Plagues of Egypt: Ancient Tradition or Literary Invention?" *ZAW* 98 (1986): 31–39.

The original plague narrative does not rest on very old traditions but was instead a composition of the exilic J, whose seven-plague sequence was later expanded by P. J's innovation was prompted by other biblical texts, which refer to curses and attribute the exodus to "signs and wonders" done by Yahweh.

449 N. Wyatt. "The Significance of the Burning Bush." *VT* 36 (1986): 361–65.

The wilderness of the exodus tradition represents the Babylonian exile, and within that context Moses is presented as a type of exile, while the burning bush symbolizes ongoing life and hope in the face of threats encountered by the exilic community. These traditions, and the larger J narrative within which they lie, are therefore exilic compositions.

450 S. Kreuzer. "430 Jahre, 400 Jahre oder 4 Generationen—Zu den Zeitangaben über den Ägyptenaufenthalt der 'Israeliten.'" *ZAW* 98 (1986): 199–210.

Explores the differing schemes by which the Pentateuch refers to the duration of the Egyptian sojourn as 430 years, 400 years, and 4 generations (cf. Gen. 15; Exod. 12:40–41).

451 F. E. Deist. "Who Is to Blame: Pharaoh, Yahweh, or Circumstance? On Human Responsibility, and Divine Ordinance." Pp. 91–112 in *Exodus 1–15: Text and Context.* Edited by J. J. Burden. Pretoria: Old Testament Society of South Africa, 1987.

The motif of Pharaoh's hardened heart reflects three different layers of material. J emphasized Pharaoh's individual responsibility, D warned that continuing disobedience could result in

Yahweh's hardening of Pharaoh's heart, and P viewed the deity
as completely sovereign over the human heart.

452 L. M. Muntingh. "Egypt as a Hermeneutical Principle in
the Theology behind the Plagues of Egypt." Pp. 113–46 in
Exodus 1–15: Text and Context. Edited by J. J. Burden. Pretoria: Old Testament Society of South Africa, 1987.

The plague narratives reflect God's universal sovereignty over
all nations rather than God's victory in a specific, Egyptian historical context. Hence, in Exodus, the name "Egypt" is a glyph
that represents all oppressive nations.

453 M. L. Brenner. *The Song of the Sea: Ex 15:1–21.* BZAW 195.
Berlin and New York: de Gruyter, 1991.

Although Exod. 15 is often believed one of the oldest portions
of the Hebrew Bible, it was composed by Levites during the
postexilic period.

454 L. Eslinger. "Freedom or Knowledge? Perspective and Purpose in the Exodus Narrative (Exodus 1–15)." *JSOT* 52
(1991): 43–60.

Although commonly co-opted as a source of liberation theology
(freedom from oppression), the more important concern in the
Exodus narrative is to promote knowledge of divine omnipotence.

455 J. G. Janzen. "Song of Moses, Song of Miriam: Who Is Sec-
onding Whom?" *CBQ* 54 (1992): 211–20.

Contrary to some theorists, who see both a Song of Moses and
a Song of Miriam in Exod. 15, Janzen views the "Song of
Moses" in 15:1–18 as Miriam's song.

456 J. D. Currid. "Why Did God Harden Pharaoh's Heart?"
BRev 9, no. 6 (1993): 46–51.

In Egyptian tradition, the "heart" was evaluated for purity before the deceased was admitted to a blissful afterlife. God hardened Pharaoh's heart as an expression of divine sovereignty and
to imply the impurity of Pharaoh's heart.

457 W. H. Propp. "That Bloody Bridegroom (Exodus iv 24–6)."
VT 43 (1993): 495–518.

Yahweh sought to kill Moses in Exod. 4 because Moses had
murdered an Egyptian. This was averted when Zipporah cir-
cumcised Gershom and touched the bloody foreskin to the
penis of Moses, thus atoning for his guilt.

458 N. L. Collins. "Evidence in the Septuagint of a Tradition in
Which the Israelites Left Egypt without Pharaoh's Con-
sent." *CBQ* 56 (1994): 442–48.

The Greek translation of Exod. 3:21–22 and 11:2–3 reflects a
Hebrew *Vorlage* that is consistent with the notion that one tra-

dition in ancient Israel had the Hebrews leaving Egypt covertly rather than by expulsion.

459 E. L. Greenstein. "The Firstborn Plague and the Reading Process." Pp. 555–68 in *Pomegranates and Golden Bells: Studies in Biblical, Jewish, and Near Eastern Ritual, Law, and Literature in Honor of Jacob Milgrom.* Edited by D. P. Wright, D. N. Freedman, and A. Hurvitz. Winona Lake, Ind.: Eisenbrauns, 1995.

Firstborn males belong to Yahweh in Israelite theology and must be sacrificially redeemed. The death of Egypt's unredeemed firstborn at Passover therefore expresses Yahweh's divine sovereignty over Egypt.

460 J. Van Seters. "A Context of Magicians? The Plague Stories in P." Pp. 569–80 in *Pomegranates and Golden Bells: Studies in Biblical, Jewish, and Near Eastern Ritual, Law, and Literature in Honor of Jacob Milgrom.* Edited by D. P. Wright, D. N. Freedman, and A. Hurvitz. Winona Lake, Ind.: Eisenbrauns, 1995.

P's five "plague" stories (rod to snake; water to blood; frogs; gnats; boils) reflect a "contest" motif in which Moses and Aaron bested Pharaoh's magicians and were thus legitimized before the king. P's integration of these stories into J indicates that these five stories never existed as an independent P source.

461 T. L. Thompson. "How Yahweh Became God: Exodus 3 and 6 and the Heart of the Pentateuch." *JSOT* 68 (1995): 57–74.

The "revelations" of the divine name in Exod. 3 and 6 reflect a postexilic monotheism that was inclusive of polytheism. In Exod. 6, for instance, the local Levantine deity, Yahweh, was interpreted as truly divine by associating his name with the divine presence ("I will be with you").

462 R. B. Allen. "The Bloody Bridegroom in Exodus 4:24–26." *BSac* 153 (1996): 259–69.

Zipporah did not cast Gershom's foreskin at the feet of Moses but toward the deity. Out of frustration she calls God her blood relative by means of the enforced circumcision of her son.

463 M. Vervenne. "Exodus Expulsion and Exodus Flight: The Interpretation of a Crux Critically Examined." *JNSL* 22, no. 2 (1996): 45–58.

Many scholars (e.g., M. Noth and R. de Vaux) believe that the exodus tradition existed in two forms, a story of flight and a story of expulsion. Vervenne argues that the flight thesis stems from a misunderstanding of Exod. 14:5. There is only one exodus tradition, and its theme is Israel's expulsion from Egypt.

464   T. J. Lehane. "Zipporah and the Passover." *JBQ* 24 (1996): 46–50.

The divine warning "I will kill your firstborn son" (Exod. 4:23) was directed toward Egypt but also included Moses' uncircumcised son Gershom. God therefore sought to kill Gershom, not Moses, in 4:24. Zipporah averted this consequence by circumcising Gershom, thus bringing both Gershom and herself into a covenant relationship with Yahweh.

465   S. B. Noegel. "Moses and Magic: Notes on the Book of Exodus." *JANESCU* 24 (1996): 45–59.

Exod. 4–15 reflects intimate familiarity with Egyptian religious tradition and was composed as a polemic against Egyptian magical practices.

466   E. Carpenter. "Exodus 18: Its Structure, Style, Motifs and Function in the Book of Exodus." Pp. 91–108 in *A Biblical Itinerary: In Search of Method, Form, and Content (Essays in Honor of George W. Coats).* Edited by E. E. Carpenter. JSOTSup 240. Sheffield: Sheffield Academic Press, 1997.

Exod. 18 is a coherent narrative that introduces us to the region of Sinai. In doing so, this chapter separates the book into two parts, with vv. 1–12 providing an epilogue for Exod. 2–17 and vv. 13–27 providing the prologue for Exod. 19–40.

467   A. Phillips and L. Phillips. "The Origin of 'I Am' in Exodus 3.14." *JSOT* 78 (1998): 81–84.

Yahweh's name, which appears as *'ehyeh* in Exod. 3:13–15, can be explained as a redactional addition inspired by Hos. 1:9. While in Hos. 1:9 Yahweh says to the north, "You are not my people," in Exod. 3:13 he says to Judah, "I will be" your God, if you obey the covenant (Exod. 19–24).

468   C. Seitz. "The Call of Moses and the 'Revelation' of the Divine Name: Source-Critical Logic and Its Legacy." Pp. 145–67 in *Theological Exegesis: Essays in Honor of Brevard S. Childs.* Edited by C. Seitz and K. E. Greene-McCreight. Grand Rapids: Eerdmans, 1999.

The two revelations of the divine name in Exod. 3 and 6 play important roles in the effort to isolate sources in the Pentateuch. However, these two texts can be coherently related to each other in a way that raises questions about any simple and straightforward division of the Pentateuch into sources J and P.

6.5 The Sinai Pericope: Exodus 19–24

The so-called Sinai pericope recounts the great theophany on Mount Sinai and the initial covenant between Yahweh and Israel. This section includes two sets of entries, those addressing the interpretation of Exod. 19–24 and those that address the law code within this text, the Book of the Covenant (BC). For related entries, see §§5.2 and 5.3.

6.5.1 Composition and Interpretation

469 D. Patrick. "The Covenant Code Source." *VT* 27 (1977): 145–57.

> The present framework of BC (Exod. 19:3b–8; 20:22; 24:3–8) was composed in the northern kingdom to place the code within a covenant context of negotiation, revelation, and ratification. The resulting text was later combined with E, which was in turn folded into J.

470 A. Phillips. "A Fresh Look at the Sinai Pericope: Part 1." *VT* 34 (1984): 39–52; "A Fresh Look at the Sinai Pericope: Part 2." *VT* 34 (1984): 282–94.

> Contra Nicholson (#405), the Decalogue's association with the Sinai covenant is quite old. Proto-Deuteronomists during the reign of Hezekiah took up BC (Exod. 21–23) and framed it with these materials to complete Exod. 19–24; they also composed Exod. 32–34. Deut. 5 took up this Decalogue in order to lend authority to its new laws, associated with Josiah's seventh-century reforms.

471 J. Van Seters. " 'Comparing Scripture with Scripture': Some Observations on the Sinai Pericope of Exodus 9–24." Pp. 111–30 in *Canon, Theology, and Old Testament Interpretation: Essays in Honor of Brevard S. Childs.* Edited by G. M. Tucker et al. Philadelphia: Fortress, 1988.

> Contrary to the usual view, the Sinai pericope of Exod. 19–24 is based on the earlier Deuteronomic Horeb theophany (Deut. 4–5).

472 T. B. Dozeman. *God on the Mountain: A Study of Redaction, Theology, and Canon in Exodus 19–24.* SBLMS 37. Atlanta: Scholars, 1989.

> Outlines a three-phase development of Exod. 19–24 that includes preexilic (God's mountain tradition), late preexilic/exilic (Deuteronomistic), and exilic/postexilic (Priestly) contributions. Dozeman then explores the theological dimensions of

reading the sometimes divergent theologies of these three levels.

473 R. S. Hendel. "Sacrifice as a Cultural System: The Ritual Symbolism of Exodus 24,3–8." *ZAW* 101 (1989): 366–90.

The covenant ceremony in Exod. 24 suitably represents the unifying social function of the Israelite sacrificial system.

474 Z. Zevit. "The Earthen Altar Laws of Exodus 20:24–26 and Related Sacrificial Restrictions in Their Cultural Context.'" Pp. 53–62 in *Texts, Temples, and Traditions: A Tribute to Menahem Haran*. Edited by M. V. Fox et al. Winona Lake, Ind.: Eisenbrauns, 1996.

The elevated altar of Exod. 20 served a polemical function by distinguishing Yahweh from chthonic (underworld) deities.

475 Y. Avishur. "The Narrative of the Revelation at Sinai (Exod 19–24)." Pp. 197–214 in *Studies in Historical Geography and Biblical Historiography: Presented to Zecharia Kallai.* Edited by G. Galil and M. Weinfeld. VTSup 81. Leiden: Brill, 2000.

The Sinai narrative reflects two originally independent traditions, one in which God speaks to the people and another in which he speaks only to Moses.

476 S. Schenker. "La difference des peines pour les vols de bétail selon le *Code de l'Alliance* (Ex XXI,37 et XXII,3)." *RB* 107 (2000): 18–23.

The difference between the penalty prescribed in the theft law of Exod. 21:37 (400 to 500 percent) and the theft law of Exod. 22:3 (200 percent) stems from the question of premeditation. The former was premeditated and the latter was not.

6.5.2 The Book of the Covenant

477 J. W. McKay. "Exodus XXIII 1–3, 6–8: A Decalogue for the Administration of Justice in the City Gate." *VT* 21 (1971): 311–25.

A close reading of Exod. 23 reveals that vv. 1–3, 6–8 contain a Decalogue for jurisprudence at the city gates.

478 G. J. Wenham. "Legal Forms in the Book of the Covenant." *TynBul* 22 (1971): 95–102.

Offers a detailed typology of the law forms in BC. Concludes that the participial forms (e.g., "The one who does [this or that] . . .") are essentially casuistic forms (i.e., "[In the case of] the one who does [this or that] . . ."). Suggests that it is quite difficult to assign the laws to a particular context (*Sitz im Leben*) on the basis of form.

479 B. S. Jackson. "The Problem of Exod. XXI 22–5 *(IUS TALI-ONIS)*." *VT* 23 (1973): 271–304.

> The law of an injured fetus in Exod. 21:22–25 is the product of an original law that has received numerous amendments. [For a critique, see S. E. Leowenstamm, "Exodus XXI 22–25," *VT* 27 (1977): 352–60.]

480 A. M. Cooper. "The Plain Sense of Exodus 23:5." *HUCA* 59 (1988): 1–22.

> The usual translations of Exod. 23:5 reflect a prescription that Israelites must assist an enemy's animal in its distress. Here it is suggested that this text actually forbids Israelites to have contact with an enemy's animal.

481 S. Isser. "Two Traditions: The Law of Exodus 21:22–23 Revisited." *CBQ* 52 (1990): 30–45.

> Discusses two ancient interpretive traditions concerning Exod. 21:22–23. One tradition views Exod. 21:22 as referring to accidental injury of a fetus and 21:23 as referring to injury of the mother. Another interpretive tradition reads 21:23 as referring, not to the mother, but to the case of a fully formed fetus. Isser comments on ancient and modern views of the law and then concludes that the second tradition is to be preferred.

482 E. Otto. "Town and Rural Countryside in Ancient Israelite Law: Reception and Redaction in Cuneiform and Israelite Law." *JSOT* 57 (1993): 3–22.

> BC reflects legal concerns from the rural countryside but was composed using the legal drafting techniques of Near Eastern scribal culture. Israelite scribes were familiar with these techniques because law codes were included in their training curriculum.

483 J. W. Marshall. *Israel and the Book of the Covenant: An Anthropological Approach to Biblical Law.* SBLDS 140. Atlanta: Scholars, 1993.

> The features of BC commonly cited as indicators of redaction are instead indicators of the code's composition during Israel's transition from a segmentary society to statehood.

484 J. Sprinkle. *"The Book of the Covenant": A Literary Approach.* JSOTSup 171. Sheffield: Sheffield Academic Press, 1994.

> This synchronic, literary approach to BC concludes that the law code in Exod. 20:22–23:19 is a single, uniform composition.

485 C. Pressler. "Wives and Daughters, Bond and Free: Views of Women in the Slave Laws of Exodus 21.2–11." Pp. 147–72 in *Gender and Law in the Hebrew Bible and the Ancient Near East.* Edited by V. H. Matthews, B. M. Levinson, and

T. Frymer-Kensky. JSOTSup 262. Sheffield: Sheffield Academic Press, 1998.

> The laws of Exod. 21 place women under the authority of the household male, but the customary rights of women are determined by other issues, namely, role and social class.

486 T. D. Alexander. "The Composition of the Sinai Narrative in Exodus xix 1–xxiv 11." *VT* 49 (1999): 2–20.

> The Sinai pericope is best understood as a single composition that is earlier than Deuteronomy and perhaps older than the Israelite monarchy.

6.6 The Tabernacle of God: Exodus 25–40

In their present form, the tabernacle texts of Exodus include prescriptions for erecting the structure (chaps. 25–31) as well as a description of this process (chaps. 35–40). Other accoutrements of worship are also included, such as priestly clothing, temple furniture, and so on. This sequence is interrupted by Israel's well-known calf apostasy in chapters 32–34. This section is therefore divided into two parts: entries that address the tabernacle and its furnishings as well as entries concerning the golden-calf incident.

6.6.1 Ritual Prescription and Description

487 B. Levine. "The Descriptive Tabernacle Texts of the Pentateuch." *JAOS* 85 (1965): 309–18.

> The ritual descriptions in Exod. 35–39, Lev. 8–9, and Num. 7 were derived from older archival materials but have been arranged and adapted to suit P's unique presentation of Israel's historical and cultic past. [Levine has developed a general theory that descriptive rituals are often based on archival records of offerings. See "Ugaritic Descriptive Rituals," *JCS* 17 (1963): 105–11; "Descriptive Ritual Texts from Ugarit: Some Formal and Functional Features of the *Genre*," in *The Word of the Lord Shall Go Forth: Essays in Honor of David Noel Freedman*, ed. C. L. Meyers and M. O'Connor (Winona Lake, Ind.: Eisenbrauns, 1983), 467–75.]

488 V. W. Rabe. "The Identity of the Priestly Tabernacle." *JNES* 25 (1966): 132–34.

> The priestly tabernacle in Exod. 25–31, 35–40 is commonly believed too awkward and elaborate for an itinerant wilderness setting. J. Wellhausen concluded that it was a retrojection of the Solomonic temple into the wilderness period while

M. Haran said the same with regard to the Shiloh sanctuary. A better view, proffered by F. M. Cross, is that the tabernacle was based on David's tent of Yahweh.

489 E. Lipinski. "Urim and Thummim." *VT* 20 (1970): 495–96.
Mesopotamian parallels confirm that the *urim* and *thummim* were originally two stones that provided a "yes" or "no" answer.

490 P. J. Kearney. "Creation and Liturgy: The P Redaction of Ex 25–40." *ZAW* 89 (1977): 375–87.
P's account of the tabernacle's construction is built on the same threefold creation–fall–restoration pattern that he introduced into Genesis. This was accomplished by framing the JE apostasy story of Exod. 32–34 (the fall) with a seven-speech presentation of the temple plan in Exod. 25–31 (the creation; cf. Gen. 1) and with a final construction of the tabernacle in Exod. 35–40 (the restoration). This pattern reflects an exilic hope for the restoration of sacrifices in Jerusalem.

491 R. E. Friedman. "The Tabernacle in the Temple." *BA* 43 (1980): 241–48.
Various sources, including the Deuteronomistic History, attest to the existence of the tabernacle in the preexilic period. This precludes the idea that P invented the tabernacle concept.

492 J. M. de Tarragon. "Le *Kapporet* est-elle une fiction ou un element du cult Tardif?" *RB* 88 (1981): 5–12.
According to the Deuteronomistic sources, the ark of the Solomonic temple was a simple box placed between large wooden reliefs of cherubims on the temple walls. In the postexilic period, in the absence of these reliefs, P incorporated the cherubims into a more elaborate ark cover (*kapporet*) in order to serve as the object of the *kipper* atonement ritual.

493 V. Hurowitz. "The Priestly Account of Building the Tabernacle." *JAOS* 105 (1985): 21–30.
Since Wellhausen, P's account of the tabernacle's design, construction, and dedication/celebration (Exod. 25–31, 35–40; Lev. 8–10; Num. 7) has often been viewed as the product of lengthy traditio-historical expansion of an original tabernacle tradition (Exod. 25–29; 39:42–43; Lev. 9). However, a comparison of this text with biblical (1 Kings 5–9) and Near Eastern (Old Babylonian and Ugaritic) texts suggests that the text is a single, coherent composition.

494 W. Johnstone. "Reactivating the Chronicles Analogy in Pentateuchal Studies with Special Reference to the Sinai Pericope in Exodus." *ZAW* 99 (1987): 16–37.
Just as Chronicles sought to revise Israel's history as presented in Samuel–Kings, so too did D and P revise Exod. 19–40.

495 V. Hurowitz. "Salted Incense—Exodus 30,35; Maqlu VI 111–113; IX 118–120." *Bib* 68 (1987): 178–94.

Salt was used in the Mesopotamian *Maqlu* exorcism ritual in order to influence the rate of burning. It was perhaps used in Israelite incense for the same reason.

496 C. Houtman. "On the Pomegranates and the Golden Bells of the High Priest's Mantle." *VT* 40 (1990): 223–27.

Decorative fruit and bells worn by the high priest alerted the deity to his presence in the sanctuary and so prepared the way for atoning rituals.

497 W. Horowitz and V. Hurowitz. "Urim and Thummim in Light of a Psephomancy Ritual from Assur (LKA 137)." *JNES* 21 (1992): 95–115.

Provides a transliteration, translation, and discussion of a psephomancy text (divination using black and white stones) published in 1953 (LKA 137). This text appears to be the closest Near Eastern parallel to the Israelite *urim* and *thummim.*

498 C. Houtman. "On the Function of the Holy Incense (Exodus xxx 34–8) and the Sacred Anointing Oil (xxx 22–33)." *VT* 42 (1992): 458–65.

The odors associated with human presence and biological functions can render the sacred precinct unclean. Incense and the use of anointing oil compensated for this by creating a distinct fragrance in the holy precinct. Prohibitions against the use of holy incense outside of the tabernacle reinforced the distinction between the sacred and profane.

499 D. E. Fleming. "Mari's Large Public Tent and the Priestly Tent Sanctuary." *VT* 50 (2000): 484–98.

Scholars commonly assume that the priestly tabernacle is merely an imaginary retrojection of the temple structure into the past. Evidence from Mari (ca. eighteenth century B.C.E.) suggests, however, that similar tent structures were used in other nearby cultures.

500 F. M. Cross. "The Priestly Tabernacle and the Temple of Solomon." Pp. 84–95 in *From Epic to Canon: History and Literature in Ancient Israel.* Baltimore and London: Johns Hopkins University Press, 2000.

P's postexilic tabernacle plan in Exod. 26 was adopted from older sources in the temple archive.

501 M. M. Homan. "The Divine Warrior in His Tent: A Military Model for Yahweh's Tabernacle." *BRev* 16, no. 6 (2000): 22–33, 55.

The tabernacle plan in Exod. 26 is similar to, and may have been derived from, the plans used in Egyptian military camps.

502 K. A. Kitchen. "The Desert Tabernacle: Pure Fiction or Plausible Account?" *BRev* 16, no. 6 (2000): 14–21.

The biblical tabernacle is comparable to shrines from Bronze Age Egypt and is therefore plausibly understood as historically accurate.

6.6.2 The Golden Calf in Context: Exodus 32–34

This text presents us with two problems. First, what is the purpose and message of this episode in the narrative? Second, after the golden-calf incident, the "tent of the meeting" (= tabernacle?) was removed to a place "outside the camp." Because the tabernacle did not yet exist in this narrative context, it is sometimes suggested that Exod. 32–34 interrupts the tabernacle prescriptions/descriptions in Exod. 25–40. Some scholars believe that the tabernacle pericope was inserted around Exod. 32–34, while others believe that Exod. 32–34 was inserted into the tabernacle pericope. This second possibility has prompted an active discussion about the purpose of this insertion.

503 M. Aberbach and L. Smolar. "Aaron, Jeroboam, and the Golden Calves." *JBL* 86 (1967): 129–40.

The precise parallels between the account of Aaron's golden calf in Exodus and Jeroboam's golden calves in Kings suggest that Jeroboam imitated Aaron in order to legitimize his northern cult. However, in its present context in Exod. 32, the story presents Moses and God as opponents of calf worship.

504 J. N. Oswalt. "The Golden Calves and the Egyptian Concept of Deity." *Evangelical Quarterly* 45 (1973): 13–20.

The bull calf became a symbol of apostasy in Israel because the Egyptians conceived of Amon-Re as both an invisible, transcendent god and as a bull. The bull therefore became a symbol of religion that conceives of Yahweh in physical, idolatrous terms.

505 R. W. L. Moberly. *At the Mountain of God: Story and Theology in Exodus 32–34.* JSOTSup 22. Sheffield: JSOT, 1983.

Exod. 32–34 reflects an ancient and coherent unity that cannot be explained using redactional tools.

506 H. C. Brichto. "The Worship of the Golden Calf: A Literary Analysis of a Fable on Idolatry." *HUCA* 54 (1983): 1–44.

Exod. 32–34 is a philosophical fable addressing the offense of idolatry in a context of religious iconoclasm.

507 J. G. Janzen. "The Character of the Calf and Its Cult in Exodus 32." *CBQ* 52 (1990): 597–607.

The golden calf was Israel's attempt to present Yahweh in a tangible form that would threaten its enemies.

508 D. E. Gowan. "Changing God's Mind." Pp. 90–104 in *Preaching Biblical Texts: Expositions by Jewish and Christian Scholars*. Edited by F. C. Holmgren and H. E. Schaalman. Grand Rapids: Eerdmans, 1995.

The depiction of God changing his mind in Exod. 32:7–14 is not anthropomorphism but is instead a theological statement about the nature of God.

509 S. Bar-On. "The Festival Calendars in Exodus xxiii 14–19 and xxxiv 8–26." *VT* (1998): 161–95.

The festival calendar of Exod. 34:18–26 is a late revision of the older calendar in Exod. 23:14–19. This calls into question the traditional attribution of Exod. 34:18–26 to an early J source (Exod. 23:14–19 is often attributed to E).

510 T. B. Dozeman. "Making Moses and Mosaic Authority in Torah." *JBL* 119 (2000): 21–45.

The shining face of Moses in Exod. 34:29–35 reflects a pre-Priestly attempt to elevate the lawgiver's status as God's chosen representative. Later Priestly editors attempted to transfer this image of God's glory from Moses to the tabernacle.

7

Leviticus

In its final form, the Book of Leviticus reflects a very clear structure: (1) manual of sacrifices (chaps. 1–7); (2) ordination of priests (chaps. 8–9); (3) manual of impurities (chaps. 11–15); (4) Day of Atonement (chap. 16); (5) Holiness Code (chaps. 17–26); and (6) redemption of vows (chap. 27). The entries in this section are arranged accordingly. Related materials appear in §§5.2.5, 6.6, and 8.5.

7.1 General Discussions

511 J. Milgrom. "Israel's Sanctuary: The Priestly 'Picture of Dorian Gray.'" *RB* 83 (1976): 390–99.

In both Israel and the Near East, uncleanness was viewed as a physical miasma (aerial substance) that was attracted to the sacred and that could penetrate to it from a distance. While the Near East viewed this miasma as demonic, Israel conceived of it as impersonal.

512 N. Kiuchi. *The Purification Offering in the Priestly Literature: Its Meaning and Interpretation.* JSOTSup 56. Sheffield: JSOT Press, 1988.

The so-called sin offering (*hatt'at*) functioned to purify both the temple sanctum and people from impurities that arose from ceremonial uncleanness as well as from moral fault.

513 R. P. Knierem. *Text and Concept in Leviticus 1:1–9: A Case in Exegetical Method.* FAT 2. Tübingen: Mohr Siebeck, 1992.

Concludes that we cannot know the extent to which actual cultic and ritual activities adhered, or did not adhere, to the ritual prescriptions of the biblical text.

514 M. Douglas. "Atonement in Leviticus." *JSQ* 1 (1993/94):
109–30.

> Impurity concerns in Leviticus do not reflect an obsessive and di-
> visive ideology but rather provide the structure within which
> impurities are atoned for and the community's unity is pre-
> served.

515 J. F. A. Sawyer, ed. *Reading Leviticus: A Conversation with
Mary Douglas.* JSOTSup 227. Sheffield: Sheffield Academic
Press, 1996.

> A collection of essays that address the composition, ritual ide-
> ology, and historical contexts of Leviticus. Includes respon-
> dents to the essays.

✓ **516** W. Warning. *Literary Artistry in Leviticus.* Biblical Interpretation 35. Leiden: Brill, 1999.

> The Book of Leviticus includes thirty-seven divine speeches
> that have been carefully organized to frame God's Yom Kippur
> speech in Lev. 16.

7.2 Composition, Authorship, and Context

These entries supplement those found in chapter 3.

517 A. G. Auld. "Leviticus at the Heart of the Pentateuch?" Pp.
40–51 in *Reading Leviticus: A Conversation with Mary
Douglas.* Edited by J. F. A. Sawyer. JSOTSup 227. Sheffield:
Sheffield Academic Press, 1996.

> Against M. Douglas, who argues that Leviticus is a self-stand-
> ing composition, Auld asserts that Leviticus was composed as
> an addendum to Exodus and that Numbers was in turn ap-
> pended to this Exodus–Leviticus composition.

518 R. Rendtorff. "Is It Possible to Read Leviticus as a Separate
Book?" Pp. 22–35 in *Reading Leviticus: A Conversation
with Mary Douglas.* Edited by J. F. A. Sawyer. JSOTSup
227. Sheffield: Sheffield Academic Press, 1996.

> Agrees with M. Douglas that Leviticus has a coherent structure
> and can be read as a single book, but emphasizes as well that
> Leviticus has been integrated into the Pentateuch and can only
> be fully appreciated when read within this broader literary
> context.

519 M. Douglas. *Leviticus as Literature.* Oxford: University
Press, 1999.

> Leviticus was structured mnemonically to assist the commu-
> nity in memorizing the behaviors prescribed as appropriate for
> cultic life. Douglas modifies her older theory—that animals
> were classified as unclean because they were detestable—in

favor of the view that eating them was forbidden in order to protect them.

7.3 The Manual of Offerings: Interpreting Leviticus 1–7

Scholars commonly suppose that this section of Leviticus originated as an independent manual of sacrifices (e.g., D. W. Baker [#529]), but this is not certain. The most pressing interpretive issues regard the various types of sacrifices and their significance. The usual interpretive strategy is to construct a ritual system using the regulations that can in turn be used to interpret the sacrifices. Ritual scholars have recently criticized this "systems approach." See C. Bell, *Ritual: Perspectives and Dimensions* (Oxford: Oxford University Press, 1997); and F. Staal, "The Meaninglessness of Ritual," *Numen* 26 (1974): 2–22. For related entries, see §5.2.5.

520 J. Milgrom. "The Cultic שגגה and Its Influence in Psalms and Job." *JQR* 58 (1967): 115–25.

In the Priestly writings, *shegagah* ("error") refers to offenses committed due to either negligence or ignorance.

521 A. F. Rainey. "The Order of Sacrifices in Old Testament Ritual Texts." *Bib* 51 (1970): 485–98.

While the descriptive texts in Lev. 8–9 reflect a ritual progression from sin- to burnt- to peace-offerings, in Num. 7, 28, and 29 the progression is burnt-, sin-, and peace-offerings. Administrative texts like Lev. 1–7 are more reliable for reconstructing actual ritual practice, and this text provides two other progressions.

522 J. Milgrom. "Sin-Offering or Purification-Offering?" *VT* 21 (1971): 237–39.

The *hatta't* sacrifice does not purify the offerer, as is often assumed, but instead cleanses or decontaminates the sanctuary. This prevents an accumulation of impurity that might cause the deity to abandon the sanctuary and Israel. [Due to Milgrom's influence, most scholars now describe the "sin-offering" as the "purification-" or "purgation-offering."]

523 J. Milgrom. "The Alleged Wave-Offering in Israel and in the Ancient Near East." *IEJ* 22 (1972): 33–38.

Hebrew philology and comparative evidence from the Near East show that the *tenufa* (so-called wave-offering) is a ritual in which offerings are vertically elevated to the deity rather than horizontally "waved" before the deity.

524 J. Milgrom. "The Priestly Doctrine of Repentance." *RB* 82 (1975): 186–205.

According to P (Lev. 5:20–26), repentance expressed in guilt, confession, and the offering of *'asham* ("guilt-offering") reduces a capital crime to an inadvertent sin that can be expiated.

525 J. Milgrom. "Two Kinds of *ḥaṭṭā't*." *VT* 26 (1976): 333–37.

Hebrew law prescribes two different procedures for the sin-offering (*hatta't*), one in which the blood is daubed on the outer altar and its meat eaten by priests and one in which the blood is daubed on the inner incense altar and sprinkled before the veil, but the meat is not consumed. The eaten *hatta't* purges the outer altar from inadvertent sins of the individual while the uneaten *hatta't* purges the inner altar from presumptuous sins or from the inadvertent sins of the priests or the community.

526 D. Davies. "An Interpretation of Sacrifice in Leviticus." *ZAW* 89 (1977): 387–99.

Israel's social and religious order was structured and preserved through its sacrificial system. This phenomenon closely corresponds to the important anthropological theories of H. Hubert and M. Mauss.

527 M. J. Geller. "The Šurpu Incantations and Lev 5:1–6." *Journal of Semitic Studies* 25 (1980): 181–92.

Lev. 5:1–6 and the Mesopotamian *Šurpu* rituals reflect similar attempts to deal with the negative consequences of breaking solemnly sworn oaths.

528 J. Milgrom. "The Graduated *ḥaṭṭā't* of Leviticus 5:1–13." *JAOS* 103 (1983): 249–54.

The sin-offering (*hatta't*) prescriptions in Lev. 4 and 5 are separate ritual laws. The first relates to the different means of accomplishing the sacrifice while the second addresses the social class of the offerer. The graduated *hatta't* in chapter 5 addresses the situation in which one has neglected to remove impurity, for the retention of impurity is more dangerous to Israel's connection with the deity than the initial contagion.

529 D. W. Baker. "Leviticus 1–7 and the Punic Tariffs: A Form Critical Comparison." *ZAW* 99 (1987): 188–97.

Comparison with Punic ritual prescriptions and internal evidence suggest that Lev. 1–7 originated as a reference inscription for offerers and temple officials. There is no reason why this reference work could not date to the pre-monarchic period that the text claims as its *Sitz im Leben*.

530 N. Zohar. "Repentance and Purification: The Significance and Semantics of חטאת in the Pentateuch." *JBL* 107 (1988): 609–18.

Critiques Milgrom's thesis (#525) that only the sanctuary is purified by *hatta't* rituals and that the sinner is purified by his repentance. Concludes instead that the spiritual and ritual aspects are integrally related, as is indicated by the efficacy of blood in achieving atonement and the transference of contamination to the sacrificial animal.

7.4 The Priestly Ordination: Interpreting Leviticus 8–9

See related entries in §§3.2.3 (esp. Gorman [#88]), 5.2.5, and elsewhere in Leviticus. For additional reading, see the commentaries.

531 F. H. Gorman, Jr. "Priestly Rituals of Founding: Time, Space, and Status." Pp. 47–64 in *History and Interpretation: Essays in Honour of John H. Hayes.* JSOTSup 173. Sheffield: JSOT, 1993.

> The creation story of Gen. 1:1–2:4a, the construction of the tabernacle (Exod. 40:16–38), and the Priestly ordination of Lev. 8–9 are similar rituals that create sacred time, space, and status. This reflects P's view that the world was founded through ritual and that ritual acts of founding are central to P's understanding of history.

532 G. A. Klingbeil. *A Comparative Study of the Ritual of Ordination as Found in Leviticus 8 and Emar 369.* Lewiston, N.Y.: Mellen, 1998.

> Highlights both similarities and differences between the Israelite and Emar ordination rituals. Primary focus is on the issues of symbolic meaning and social function. Includes a very useful introduction to ritual studies.

7.5 Manual of Impurities: Interpreting Leviticus 10–15

Scholars commonly suppose that this portion of Leviticus originated separately as a manual of impurities.

533 M. Douglas. "The Abominations of Leviticus." Pp. 41–57 in *Purity and Danger: An Analysis of Pollution and Taboo.* London: Routledge & Kegan Paul, 1966.

> Classification of clean and unclean animals in Lev. 11 follows two key patterns: (1) clean animals are those similar to domesticated species; and (2) clean animals are equipped with the right kind of locomotion (e.g., fish with fins and scales are suited for water and hence are clean, but lobsters with legs are not suited for water and hence are unclean). Observation of these dietary laws gives tangible expression to the abstract notions of God's oneness, purity and perfection.

534 W. L. Moran. "The Literary Connection Between Lv 11,13–19 and Dt 14,18." *CBQ* 28 (1966): 271–77.

> Deut. 14's list of ten unclean birds was used as a source in Lev.

11's list of twenty unclean birds. But form criticism shows that the ten additional species added to Lev. 11 were then added back into Deut. 14, so that both texts include twenty species in their final form.

535 J. C. H. Laughlin. "The 'Strange Fire' of Nadab and Abihu." *JBL* 95 (1976): 559–65.

Priestly law prescribed that the altar fire should burn continually (Lev. 6:8–13 = MT 6:1–6). In Lev. 10, Nadab and Abihu failed to use this holy fire and sinned by bringing into the tabernacle a fire that had been kindled outside of the holy precinct. This story reflects P's polemic against postexilic Persian practices, which allowed incense and fire to be used in this way.

536 G. Robinson. "The Prohibition of Strange Fire in Ancient Israel." *VT* 28 (1978): 301–17.

Although Exod. 35:3a and Num. 25:32–36 originally prohibited "strange fire" (i.e., strange incense) to protect the cult from Canaanite influences, when the threat of idolatry had passed the word "strange" was deleted from Exod. 35:2 and the phrase "on the Sabbath day" was added. [This entry appears in this section because of its implications for the Nadab/Abihu incident in Lev. 10.]

537 J. Wilkinson. "Leprosy and Leviticus: A Problem of Semantics and Translation." *Scottish Journal of Theology* 31 (1978): 153–66.

Although the Hebrew term ṣara'at is usually translated "leprosy," this is misleading because the word includes a range of human skin symptoms as well as various types of mold, rot, and mildew that might grow on inanimate objects.

538 P. Segal. "The Divine Verdict of Leviticus x 3." *VT* 39 (1989): 91–95.

God's swift destruction of Nadab and Abihu was an act of grace that prevented further contamination of the sanctuary and, hence, further punishment for Israel.

539 G. J. Wenham. "Why Does Sexual Intercourse Defile (Lev 15:18)?" *ZAW* 95 (1983): 432–34.

According to Levitical law, only that which corresponds to the normal life patterns of wholeness and integrity is viewed as clean. The loss of life fluids, such as blood and semen, therefore renders worshipers impure until they can recover from the loss.

540 S. Meier. "House Fungus: Mesopotamia and Israel (Lev 14:33–53)." *RB* 96 (1989): 184–92.

Both Israelite and Mesopotamian societies were concerned by the presence of household fungus and addressed this problem through ritual. However, in Israel the fungus itself was the potential threat, while in Mesopotamia the fungus portended evil for the home's owner. Consequently, the object of ritual cleansing in Israel was the house, while in Mesopotamia holy water was applied to the house's owner.

541 E. Firmage. "The Biblical Dietary Laws and the Concept of Holiness." Pp. 177–208 in *Studies in the Pentateuch*. Edited by J. A. Emerton. VTSup 41. Leiden: E. J. Brill, 1990.

The dietary rules of Lev. 11 do not stem from preexisting taboos but from normal human dietary patterns. Contrary to the usual view, it is likely that the dietary rules of Lev. 11 are older than those in Deut. 14.

542 M. Douglas. "The Forbidden Animals in Leviticus." *JSOT* 59 (1993): 3–23.

The forbidden animals of Lev. 11 include vulnerable herbivores as well as young or disfigured animals. These do not symbolize various virtues, as is commonly suggested, but represent instead human victims of injustice, such as orphans, widows, and the poor. Holiness is incompatible with predatory behavior.

543 J. Milgrom. "The Rationale for Biblical Impurity." *JANESCU* 22 (1993): 107–11.

The bodily impurities of Lev. 12–15 stem from the same source: death. Flows of blood and semen are loses of life force and hence represent death. Skin diseases similarly represent the passing of the body and hence the advance of death.

544 R. Whitekettle. "Leviticus 12 and the Israelite Woman: Ritual Process, Liminality, and the Womb." *ZAW* 107 (1995): 393–408.

The uncleanness of postpartum women stems from the fact that they are unable to conceive and bear children immediately following birth. All discharges of the reproductive system were viewed as interruptions of fertility and, hence, by priestly law, as unclean pathologies.

545 J. Magonet. " 'But if It Is a Girl, She Is Unclean for Twice Seven Days . . .': The Riddle of Leviticus 12:5." Pp. 144–52 in *Reading Leviticus: A Conversation with Mary Douglas*. Edited by J. F. A. Sawyer. JSOTSup 227. Sheffield: Sheffield Academic Press, 1996.

Maternal hormones can cause newborn girls to experience vaginal bleeding. The blood of the mother and the infant girl therefore produce a period of uncleanness that is double that of a mother bearing a boy.

546 M. A. Greenberg. "The True Sin of Nadab and Abihu." *JBQ* 26 (1998): 263–67.

Nadab and Abihu were the priests who uttered the words, "these are the gods who brought you out of Egypt," during the golden-calf episode of Exod. 32. Their entry into the Yahweh's presence in Lev. 10 therefore prompted divine punishment upon this unatoned sin.

7.6 The Day of Atonement in Leviticus 16

The disposal ritual in Lev. 16 must be read in light of the larger sacrificial and ritual context of Israel (§§5.2.5, 7.5, 8.5). There are also striking similarities between this ritual and Near Eastern disposal rituals. For an important comparative text, see *ANET* 331–34. For comparative discussions, see Ch. Cohen (#80) and D. P. Wright (#368).

547 C. L. Feinberg. "The Scapegoat of Leviticus Sixteen." *BSac* 115 (1959): 320–33.

Is the *azazel* of Lev. 16 a place, a thing, or a person? All of these options are inadequate. Both goats in Lev. 16—including the one destined for *azazel*—are sin-offerings. One was sacrificed, and the other symbolically carried Israel's sins into the wilderness.

548 R. A. Soloff. "Yom Kippur: Cover-Up or Plea for Probation?" *JBQ* 25 (1997): 86–89.

The Day of Atonement granted protective cover from sins of the previous year and so allowed for another year "on probation."

549 I. Zatelli. "The Origin of the Biblical Scapegoat Ritual: The Evidence of Two Eblaite Texts." *VT* 48 (1998): 254–63.

The Eblaites practiced a royal wedding preparation ritual in which the temple was cleansed prior to the arrival of the deities Kura and Barama and of the king and queen. In a manner similar to the Israelite scapegoat, in the Eblaite ritual a goat with a silver bracelet on its neck was released toward the "steppe of Alini."

550 C. Carmichael. "The Origin of the Scapegoat Ritual." *VT* 50 (2000): 167–82.

Contrary to common opinion, the Day of Atonement scapegoat ritual in Lev. 16 does not derive from a Near Eastern prototype but is instead a uniquely Israelite tradition.

7.7 The Holiness Code: Leviticus 17–26

In 1877, A. Kloserman coined the term *Heiligkeitsgesetz* (Holiness Code) to describe Lev. 17–26 because of its repetitive emphasis on holiness. Because of similarities between HC and the exilic prophet Ezekiel, scholars commonly view this law code as stemming from the early exilic period. There are of course dissenters from this view. Some scholars view HC as pre-exilic, while others argue that it is a much more extensive layer of material found not only in Lev. 17–26 but also in other texts. Still others argue that HC cannot be differentiated from P or that it is a late redaction of P. For additional related entries, see §5.2.

7.7.1 General Discussions

551 G. von Rad. "Form-Criticism of the Holiness Code." Pp. 25–36 in *Studies in Deuteronomy*. SBT 9. Chicago: Henry Regnery, 1953.
    HC's laws originated as sermons and then were presented as divine instructions uttered alternately to the people and to the priests. Its use of parenesis is similar to Deuteronomy's, so that neither is in this regard unique.

552 W. Kornfeld. *Studien zum Heiligkeitsgesetz*. Vienna: Verlag Herder, 1952.
    Includes two studies, a form-critical study of HC's laws and a study of HC's marriage laws and laws governing sexual relationships. Isolates three categories of casuistic genres (true casuistic, relative form, and participial form) and three categories of apodictic genres (proscriptive imperfect, jussive form, and "mixed form"). Only the "true" casuistic forms reflect Near Eastern jurisprudence; the remaining laws are native Israelite forms.

553 H. G. Reventlow. *Das Heiligkeitsgesetz: Formgeschichtlich untersucht*. Neukirchen: Neukirchener Verlag, 1961.
    The earliest core of HC is a Decalogue in chapter 19, around which grew the apodictic collection of laws in chapters 17–20. Early in the process, the blessings and curses of chapter 26 were added to this law collection, and later additions in chapters 21–25 completed the code. The *Sitz im Leben* of the code, from its earliest Decalogue to final form, was the annual covenant festival as envisioned by Alt, Noth, and von Rad.

554 J. Magonet. "The Structure and Meaning of Leviticus 19." *HAR* 7 (1983): 151–67.
    The sequence of topics in Lev. 19 moves from humanity's relationship with God, to human relationships with each other, to human relationships with the self. Hence, holiness for the society and for the individual lies in conforming to the standards of integrity and order established by God in creation.

555 J. Joosten. "The Numeruswechsel in the Holiness Code (Lev. XVII–XXVI). Pp. 67–71 in *"Lasset uns Brücken* *bauen . . .": Collected Communications to the XVth Congress of the Organization for the Study of the Old Testament, Cambridge 1995.* Frankfurt am Main: Lang, 1998.

> Variations in singular and plural pronouns in the HC are not indices for identifying different sources or redactional material. These alternations are better understood as a rhetorical device employed by HC's author.

556 J. Milgrom. "Does H Advocate the Centralization of Worship?" *JSOT* 88 (2000): 59–76.

> Contrary to the usual view, HC (Lev. 17:1–7) does not presume that worship was limited to a single sanctuary (nor does P). The absolute ban on nonsacrificial slaughter in Lev. 17:1–7 could not have been implemented if there was only one sanctuary.

7.7.2 Interpreting the Holiness Code, Leviticus 17–26 (27)

557 O. Eissfeldt. *Molk als Opferbegriff im Punischen und Hebräischen und das Ende des Gottes Moloch.* Beiträge zur Religionsgeschichte des Altertums 3. Halle, Germany: Niemeyer, 1935.

> Although the Hebrew term *molech* (e.g., Lev. 18:21) is commonly understood to reflect a deity named Molech who received human sacrifices, Punic evidence suggests that the proper understanding of the term is *molk*, a type of infant human sacrifice.

558 J. Weingreen. "The Case of the Blasphemer." *VT* 22 (1972): 118–23.

> In what sense did the son in Lev. 24:10–16 blaspheme Yahweh? His sin was that he spoke the divine name for no purpose, that is, without good reason. A similar viewpoint is reflected in the Decalogue (cf. Exod. 20:7; Deut. 5:11).

559 J. Milgrom. "The Betrothed Slave-Girl, Lev 19:20–22." *ZAW* 89 (1977): 43–50.

> Although Hebrew law treats adultery as a capital crime, the seducer of a betrothed female slave is directed to provide a guilt-offering rather than face death. This is because the female slave was not a legal person and, hence, the act committed was not adultery.

560 R. Gnuse. "Jubilee Legislation in Leviticus: Israel's Vision of Social Reform." *Biblical Theology Bulletin* 15 (1985): 43–48.

> Drawing on influences from both BC and DC, the Jubilee laws of Lev. 25 and 27 provided images of hope to Jews in the Babylonian exile The Jubilee institution was never actually prac-

ticed but instead provided a utopian vision of society without poverty. This conclusion is suggested by the practical problems created by Jubilee implementation, in which the fiftieth year following the seventh Sabbath year (forty-ninth) creates two successive and impractical Sabbath years.

561 M. A. Zipor. "Restrictions on Marriage for Priests (Lev 21:7,13–14)." *Biblica* 68 (1987): 259–67.

Discusses the marriage rules for priests, which forbade them to marry prostitutes or divorcées and, in the case of the high priest, forbade marriage to prostitutes, divorcées, and widows but prescribed marriage to a virgin from his clan.

✓ **562** J. Day. *Molech: A God of Human Sacrifice in the Old Testament.* Cambridge: Cambridge University Press, 1989.

Contrary to Eissfeldt (#557), concludes that Molek was a West Semitic god of human sacrifice.

563 B. J. Schwartz. "The Prohibitions Concerning the 'Eating' of Blood in Leviticus 17." Pp. 34–66 in *Priesthood and Cult in Ancient Israel.* Edited by G. A. Anderson and S. M. Olyan. JSOTSup 125. Sheffield: JSOT, 1991.

Explores how and why the regulations regarding eating blood were composed, drawing insights about the nature of ritual law in Israel and about the nature of P.

564 M. A. Greenberg. "The Red Heifer Ritual: A Rational Explanation." *JBQ* 25 (1997): 44–46.

The red heifer provided the following ritual imagery: (1) third-day sprinkling reflects the three-day purification at Sinai; (2) seventh-day sprinkling reflects the Priestly isolation period; (3) burning of the heifer is reminiscent of "strange incense" offered by Nadab and Abihu (Lev. 10); and (4) burned heifer is a symbol of the golden calf, which was also burned and sprinkled with water (Exod. 32).

565 M. Hudson. "Proclaim Liberty throughout the Land: The Economic Roots of the Jubilee." *BRev* 15, no. 1 (1999): 26–33, 44.

The biblical law of Jubilee (Lev. 25) is similar to the genre of Near Eastern edicts (*misharu*) that provided debt relief and the emancipation of slaves. The primary difference is that the biblical law sought to formalize what was, in the Near East, a sporadic practice.

566 K. Grünwaldt. *Das Heiligkeitsgesetz Leviticus 17–26: Ursprüngliche Gestalt, Tradition und Theologie.* BZAW 271. Berlin: de Gruyter, 1999.

HC was composed by an educated layman as a postexilic alternative to DC. The need for this new code arose when the Jewish community returned from the exile during the Persian period.

567   J. Milgrom. "Does H Advocate the Centralization of Worship?" *JSOT* 88 (2000): 59–76.
       Contrary to the usual scholarly view, both P and HC allow for multiple sanctuaries.

7.8 Votive Laws in Leviticus 27

Ancient Israelite law permitted the redemption of things vowed to the deity by offering a monetary substitute. For additional discussions, see the commentaries. Because Lev. 26:46 appears to provide a conclusion for HC and perhaps for Leviticus as well, it is commonly assumed that Lev. 27 was added to the book after its composition.

568   R. Yaron. "Redemption of Persons in the Ancient Near East." *RIDA* 6 (1959): 155–76.
       A dated but useful discussion of redemption law in the Near East.

569   G. J. Wenham. "Leviticus 27:2–8 and the Price of Slaves." *ZAW* 90 (1978): 264–65.
       The tariff of redemption prices for persons vowed to temple service was derived from a list of Israelite slave prices.

8

Numbers

Numbers reflects the most complex structure of the Pentateuch's five books. The basic narrative movement of the book is straightforward—census, wilderness, disobedience, wilderness, census—but this scheme is everywhere interrupted with priestly rituals, laws, and regulations (Num. 5–10; 15; 17–19; 27–30; 35–36) as well as by what might be called "priestly lore" (Num. 16; 27). The Balaam story in Num. 22–24 adds yet another dimension to this interesting book. My bibliography of Numbers is organized according to the categories outlined here. However, because two of the primary elements in Numbers overlap with other books (priestly regulations and the wilderness tradition), the reader is directed to those sections for additional resources (§§5.5 and 5.2.5).

8.1 General Discussions

570 M. Douglas. *In the Wilderness: The Doctrine of Defilement in the Book of Numbers.* JSOTSup 158. Sheffield: JSOT, 1993.
> Numbers views ritual impurity as stemming from the human body and hence universalizes the source of defilement. This differs from separatist patterns in Judaism, which traced uncleanness to contact with foreigners. In the struggle to define the boundaries of Jewish identity, Numbers represents the losing side.

8.2 Composition, Authorship, and Context

These entries supplement those found above in chapter 3.

571 D. T. Olson. *The Death of the Old and the Birth of the*

New: The Framework of the Book of Numbers and the Pentateuch. BJS 71. Chico, Calif.: Scholars, 1985.

> The Book of Numbers is a single, coherent work that is carefully integrated into the Pentateuch. Its basic structure is (*a*) census; (*b*) death of the exodus generation; (*a´*) census; and (*b´*) emergence of the new conquest generation.

572 M. Douglas. "The Glorious Book of Numbers." *JSQ* 1 (1993/94): 193–226.

> Numbers is a carefully composed book that combines two strands of material—narrative and law—into a single whole.

8.3 Census Lists and Itinerary List (Numbers 1–4, 26, 33)

The Book of Numbers is framed by two censuses and also, in chapter 33, includes an itinerary of Israel's wilderness travels. Because of these texts' common status as "lists," entries regarding these texts are joined in this section.

573 G. E. Mendenhall. "The Census Lists of Numbers 1 and 29." *JBL* 77 (1959): 52–66.

> The census lists in Num. 1 and 26 reflect authentic and ancient traditions.

574 M. Barnouin. "Les Recensements du Livre des Nombres et l'Astronomie Baylonienne." *VT* 27 (1977): 280–303.

> The obviously artificial census figures in Numbers are perhaps based on Babylonian astronomy. The celestial numbers express the sacred character of the Israelites tribes.

575 R. I. Vasholz. "Military Censuses in *Numbers.*" *Prebyterion* 18 (1992): 122–25.

> On the basis of comparative neo-Assyrian evidence, Vasholz concludes that the large numbers in the censuses of Num. 1 and 26 reflect an ancient convention in which numbers were multiplied by ten.

576 E. W. Davies. "A Mathematical Conundrum: The Problem of the Large Numbers in Numbers i and xxvi." *VT* 45 (1995): 449–69.

> The large census numbers in Num. 1 and 26 are P's fictions, by which the blessings of Yahweh and the fulfillment of the patriarchal promises are expressed.

577 C. J. Humphreys. "The Number of People in the Exodus from Egypt: Decoding Mathematically the Very Large Numbers in Numbers i and xxvi." *VT* 48 (1998): 196–213.

> The Hebrew term *'lp* in the censuses of Numbers does not mean "one thousand" but "troop." Consequently, the total

number of Israelites exiting Egypt is much smaller than usually thought, about twenty thousand.

578   R. Heinzerling. "On the Interpretation of the Census Lists by C. J. Humphreys and G. E. Mendenhall." *VT* 50 (2000): 250–52.

Statistical features suggest that the census lists in Num. 1, 3, and 26 are not historical.

8.4 The Wilderness of Numbers

This section supplements the fuller list of entries in §5.5.

579   K. R. Joines. "The Bronze Serpent in the Israelite Cult." *JBL* 57 (1965): 245–56.

The *nehushtan* of 2 Kings 18:4 is unrelated to the bronze serpent of Num. 21:9. The bronze serpent was an instrument of sympathetic magic, borrowed from Egyptian tradition, while the *nehushtan* was a fertility symbol of Canaanite and Mesopotamian origin.

580   J. Van Seters. "The Conquest of Sihon's Kingdom: A Literary Examination." *JBL* 91 (1972): 182–97.

The composer of the Sihon battle in Num. 21:21–35 constructed this narrative using sources from Deut. 2:26–37 and Judg. 11:19–26. The war against Og was similarly taken from Deut. 3:1–7. The accounts in Numbers are therefore ideological compositions and are not historically valuable.

581   D. L. Christensen. "Num 21:14–15 and the Book of the Wars of Yahweh." *CBQ* 36 (1974): 359–60.

Num. 21:14–15 quotes from the "Book of Wars" because this source placed the boundary of Moab at the Arnon, thus presenting Yahweh, the Divine Warrior, poised at the borders of the Promised Land and ready for the conquest to begin.

582   G. W. Coats. "Conquest Traditions in the Wilderness Theme." *JBL* 95 (1976): 177–90.

A critical reconstruction of the history and composition of the wilderness and conquest traditions. All elements of these traditions, regardless of their histories, have become stages in a single, continuous journey.

8.5 Priestly Rituals, Regulations, and Lore

For related entries, see §§5.2.5 and 7.1–7.8.

583   B. Mazar. "The Cities of the Priests and Levites." Pp. 193–205 in *Congress Volume, Oxford, 1959.* VTSup 7. Leiden: Brill, 1960.

The Levitical cities of the Old Testament reflect Solomon's administrative consolidation of Israel, and it is likely that these cities were chosen because of their connection with Egypt's earlier administrative system.

584 M. Haran. "Studies in the Account of the Levitical Cities (Part 1)." *JBL* 80 (1961): 45–54; "Studies in the Account of the Levitical Cities (Part 2)." *JBL* 80 (1961): 156–65.

After surveying P's record of Levitical cities in part 1, reaches the following conclusions in part 2: some scholars have viewed the Levitical cities of P as utopian (Wellhausen) while others have viewed them as historical institutions (Alt, Noth, Albright). The reality lies between these extremes, for the material reflects historical-geographical realities that have been embellished with utopian ideology.

585 S. Bertman. "Tasseled Garments in the Ancient East Mediterranean." *BA* 24 (1961): 119–28.

Num. 15:37–41 prescribes that Israelites wear tasseled cloths. Ancient Near Eastern art depicts flower-like tassels on garments, particularly on the clothing of gods, rulers, and warriors. The tassel may therefore have indicated Israel's special status before God.

586 H. C. Brichto. "The Case of the *Sota* and the Reconsideration of Biblical Law." *HUCA* 46 (1975): 55–70.

Num. 5:11–31 is neither ordeal nor magic. The ritual was staged in order to protect the wife from her insanely jealous husband, who accused her of adultery without evidence.

587 J. Milgrom. "The Paradox of the Red Cow (Num XIX)." *VT* 31 (1981): 62–72.

The "red heifer" ritual is best understood as a type of sin-offering (*hatta't*) but also reflects vestiges of a pre-Israelite exorcism rite.

588 J. Milgrom. "The Levitic Town: An Exercise in Realistic Planning." *Journal of Jewish Studies* 33 (1982): 185–88.

Proposes that the biblical scheme for Levitical towns in Num. 35:1–8 is realistic rather than utopian.

589 J. Magonet. "The Korah Rebellion." *JSOT* 24 (1982): 3–25.

Korah's rebellion in Num. 16 dramatizes the problems of political and spiritual leadership that concerned its author(s). Specifically, Korah illustrates an illicit ambition to gain the priesthood in pursuit of personal power.

590 M. Fishbane. "Form and Reformulation of the Biblical Priestly Blessing." *JAOS* 103 (1983): 115–21.

The priestly blessing of Num. 6:23–27 reflects influences from Mesopotamian tradition. This blessing was later adapted and reformulated within Judaism's exegetical tradition.

591 T. Frymer-Kensky. "The Strange Case of the Suspected Sotah (Numbers v 11–31)." *VT* 34 (1984): 11–26.

> The ritual of Num. 5 addresses the serious threat that adultery posed to Israelite society. It is a "religio-legal" rite that delivers the accused woman over to God for judgment. Drinking the "water of revelation" would lead to divine punishment (a prolapsed uterus) or to divine blessing (fertility). The ritual was not an ordeal but a purgation oath that cleansed the woman.

592 D. P. Wright. "Purification from Corpse-Contamination in Numbers xxxi 19–24." *VT* 35 (1985): 213–23.

> The prescriptions in Num. 31:19–24 are based primarily on those from Num. 19 (waters of purgation). Eleazer's speech in vv. 21–23 is a later addition that extended this rule, requiring that metals be cleansed with both fire and the waters of purgation while requiring that other things be cleansed by water immersion and the waters of purgation. This reflects an attempt to bring the law into conformity with Num. 19, in which cleansing from corpse contamination required both ceremonial washing and the sprinkling of purgation water.

593 E. Neufeld. "The Red Heifer Mystery." *Dor le Dor* 18 (1989–90): 176–80.

> The red-heifer ritual of Num. 19 reflects homeopathic and contagious magic. The heifer symbolizes fertility, and its red color symbolizes blood.

594 R. I. Vasholz. "Israel's Cities of Refuge." *Presbyterion* 19 (1993): 116–18.

> Why did the death of the high priest in Num. 35:28 signal amnesty for those confined in cities of refuge? Just as the death of David signaled amnesty for Shimei in 1 Kings 2:36–38, so too did the high priest's death end a judicial era.

595 Ch. Cohen. "The Biblical Priestly Blessing (Num 6:24–26) in Light of Akkadian Parallels." *Tel Aviv* 20 (1993): 228–38.

> The priestly blessing of Num. 6 and Akkadian parallels reflect semantically equivalent idioms.

596 A. I. Baumgarten. "The Paradox of the Red Heifer." *VT* 43 (1993): 442–51.

> Why do the ashes of the red heifer purify the unclean and render unclean those who prepare them? Uncleanness arose in ancient Israel for two reasons: undue proximity to the sacred and inordinate distance from it. This differs from the view of J. Milgrom, who argues that future impurities to be absorbed by the ashes render them proleptically unclean.

597 J. Milgrom. "A Husband's Pride, a Mob's Prejudice." *BRev* 12 (1996): 21.

The ordeal of Num. 5 was prescribed in order to protect the suspected adulteress from death, because there were no witnesses to her supposed crime.

598   E. Diamond. "An Israelite Self-Offering in the Priestly Code: A New Perspective on the Nazirite." *JQR* 88 (1997): 1–18.

The Nazirite vow described in Num. 6 results in the symbolic offering of the Nazirite to God.

599   S. R. Keller. "An Egyptian Analogue to the Priestly Blessing." Pp. 338–45 in *Boundaries of the Ancient Near Eastern World: A Tribute to Cyrus H. Gordon*. Edited by M. Lubetski, C. Gottlieb, and S. Keller. JSOTSup 273. Sheffield: Sheffield Academic Press, 1998.

The priestly blessing of Num. 6:24–26 is similar in form and content to an Egyptian ritual letter from the first intermediate period. When compared to the seventh-century B.C.E. Hebrew amulets inscribed with the priestly blessing, this suggests that both the Egyptian and Hebrew texts may have served as talismans to protect the deceased in the afterlife.

600   R. T. Harris. "The Ritual of the Red Heifer." *JBQ* 26 (1998): 198–200.

Attempts to explain why the ashes of the red heifer in Num. 19 cleanse those who are unclean but make unclean those who prepare the ashes. The ashes are used to make the waters for ritual cleansing (literally, *me niddah* = "waters of menstrual uncleanness"). Because menstruation represents a minor death, the use of the cleansing water substitutes a "minor death" to cleanse from real death.

601   B. D. Haberman. "The Suspected Adulteress: A Study of Textual Embodiment." *Prooftexts* 20 (2000): 12–42.

The primary function of the *sotah* ritual in Num. 5:11–31 was to address the problem of male jealousy and to protect marriage and the patriarchal social order of ancient Israel.

8.6 The Balaam Story (Numbers 22–24)

Modern interpretations of the Balaam story are generally preoccupied with five questions: (1) What role does the story play in the narrative? (2) Why is Balaam presented as both a righteous and evil prophet? (3) What is the significance of Balaam's foreign identity? (4) What is the relationship between the biblical Balaam and the Balaam in the Deir 'Alla texts from Transjordan? and (5) What are we to make of the poetry in the Balaam pericope?

602   G. W. Coats. "Balaam: Sinner or Saint?" *Biblical Research* 18 (1973): 21–29.

The Balaam story reflects two traditions about Balaam, one positive and one negative.

603 A. Tosato. "The Literary Structure of the First Two Poems of Balaam." *VT* 29 (1979): 98–106.

The first two Balaam poems in Num. 23:7–10 and 23:18–24 are structured to reflect concentric symmetry, the first following the pattern A-B-A′ and the second A-B-C-B′-A′. This poetry was probably written in the northern kingdom during the preexilic period.

604 B. A. Levine. "The Deir 'Alla Plaster Inscriptions." *JAOS* 101 (1981): 195–205.

Translation, commentary, and discussion of the Balaam texts from Deir 'Alla.

605 J. A. Hackett. *The Balaam Text from Deir 'Alla.* HSM 31. Chico, Calif.: Scholars, 1984.

Provides a transliteration and translation of this important comparative text regarding the figure Balaam. Concludes that the text reflects an Ammonite rather than Aramaic dialect.

606 W. E. Aufrecht. "A Bibliography of the Deir 'Alla Plaster Texts." *Newsletter for Targumic and Cognate Studies,* supp. 2 (1985): 1–7.

A useful bibliographic survey of these important texts regarding the figure Balaam.

607 J. D. Safren. "Balaam and Abraham." *VT* 38 (1988): 105–13.

The portrayal of Balaam in Num. 22:22–35 is a mirror narrative of that of Abraham in Gen. 22:1–19, which seeks to demonize Balaam by portraying him as the polar opposite of Israel's faithful patriarch.

608 M. S. Moore. *The Balaam Traditions: Their Character and Development.* SBLDS 113. Atlanta: Scholars, 1990.

Why do the biblical materials portray Balaam as both a legitimate prophet of Yahweh and as a "blind seer"? The Deir 'Alla inscriptions portray a Balaam figure who is both diviner and exorcist. The ambivalence of the biblical materials reflects Israelite responses to these two roles, embracing the diviner as "religious" but rejecting the exorcist as "magical."

609 G. Savran. "Beastly Speech: Intertextuality, Balaam's Ass, and the Garden of Eden." *JSOT* 64 (1994): 33–55.

The story of Balaam alludes to and inverts various motifs and themes from the garden of Eden story and from other episodes in the Pentateuch.

610 W. C. Kaiser, Jr. "Balaam Son of Beor in Light of Deir 'Alla and Scripture: Saint or Soothsayer?" Pp. 95–106 in *"Go to the Land I Will Show You": Studies in Honor of Dwight S.*

Young. Edited by J. E. Coleson and V. H. Matthews. Winona Lake, Ind.: Eisenbrauns, 1996.

> Balaam was a historical person from Ammon and a convert to Yahwism but later joined the Midianites in their struggle against the Yahwists.

611 M. L. Barré. "The Portrait of Balaam in Numbers 22–24." *Int* 51 (1997): 254–66.

> Compares and contrasts the figure of Balaam in Num. 22–24 with the Balaam of the Aramaic Deir 'Alla inscription. Numbers presents Balaam as a prophet of God and virtually of Yahweh, while Deir 'Alla's Balaam receives and then passes on a message of destruction from the divine council. In both texts, Balaam faithfully presents his message in a spirit of mournfulness.

612 J. Van Seters. "From Faithful Prophet to Villain: Observations on the Tradition History of the Balaam Story." Pp. 126–32 in *A Biblical Itinerary: In Search of Method, Form, and Content: Essays in Honor of George W. Coats.* Edited by E. E. Carpenter. JSOTSup 240. Sheffield: Sheffield Academic Press, 1997.

> J adapted the well-known prophet Balaam to compose his narrative in Num. 22–24. This was done during the late-exilic period, for the exilic prologue of Deut. 1–3 does not know the Balaam story. While J's Balaam was a positive figure, the prophet was later vilified in P and in other postexilic traditions.

613 J. W. Wevers. "The Balaam Narrative according to the Septuagint." Pp. 133–44 in *Lectures et relectures de la Bible: Festschrift P.-M. Bogaert.* Edited by J.-M. Auwers and A. Wénin. BETL 144. Louvain: Louvain University Press; Peeters, 1999.

> The LXX translators of the Balaam story were uncomfortable with the idea that Israel's God, Yahweh, spoke to the foreign prophet Balaam. As a result, the Septuagint attempted to imply that Balaam was a prophet of "God" rather than of "Yahweh."

9

Deuteronomy

Scholars generally agree that the book found in the temple during Josiah's seventh-century reforms in Judah was some form of Deuteronomy. For many scholars, this suggests that the book should be dated to that period, while others view it as somewhat older, or at least as containing some older traditions. Another point of consensus is that Deuteronomy's structure and content are similar to Near Eastern treaties, especially first-millennium neo-Assyrian treaties. Most of the relevant entries regarding this last issue are found in §5.3.

9.1 General Discussions

614 A. C. Welch. *The Code of Deuteronomy*. London: James Clarke, 1924.

Deuteronomy originated in the northern kingdom during the period of Samuel as a polemic against Baal worship and its many pagan shrines. Through the addition of a centralization clause in Deut. 12:1–7, this law book was later adapted to serve the purposes of Josiah's reforms in seventh-century Judah.

615 G. von Rad. *Deuteronomium-Studien*. Göttingen: Vandenhoeck & Ruprecht, 1948. English translation: *Studies in Deuteronomy*. SBT 9. Chicago: Henry Regnery, 1953.

A classic collection of essays that address the form, theology, provenance, and purpose of Deuteronomy. Among other things, the collection concludes that Deuteronomy's oldest traditions originated in the north, that the book was composed by Levites during the decline of Assyria late in the Judean monarchy (ca. 701 B.C.E.), that it sought to revive Judah religiously and mili-

tarily, and that the cult-centralization program of the book is a
late layer of material associated with Josiah's reform.

616 M. Weinfeld. "Cult Centralization in Israel in the Light of
a Neo-Babylonian Analogy." *JNES* 23 (1964): 202–12.

The effort of Nabonidus to bring the gods to Babylon when fac-
ing Persian threats is similar to Josiah's cult-centralization program in the face of Assyrian threats.

617 R. E. Clements. "Deuteronomy and the Jerusalem Cult
Tradition." *VT* 15 (1965): 300–312.

Deuteronomy adapted the *bahar* ("to choose") election theology of the Davidic monarchy and its fixation with Jerusalem to
make Israel the object of election and Jerusalem the one and
only dwelling of Yahweh.

618 M. Weinfeld. "Deuteronomy: The Present State of In-
quiry." *JBL* 86 (1967): 249–62.

A historically valuable summary of scholarly consensus and
debate, as of 1967, on the Book of Deuteronomy.

619 E. W. Nicholson. *Deuteronomy and Tradition.* Philadelphia: Fortress, 1967.

Deuteronomy originated as a Josianic-era covenant law book
(late seventh century B.C.E.) and was subsequently edited after
the exile, incorporated into the Deuteronomistic History, and
then combined with the Tetrateuch to form the Pentateuch.
The original code drew on older materials and ideologies from
the northern kingdom. This code adapted Judean monarchic
tradition by making Jerusalem its focal point, but it deviated
from this tradition by emphasizing the divine election of Israel
instead of the election of the king (cf. Clements [#617]). The ar-
chitects of this reform were prophets rather than priests (von
Rad [#615]), elders (Hoppe [#643]), or wisdom scribes (Weinfeld
[#626]).

620 M. Weinfeld. *Deuteronomy and the Deuteronomic School.*
Reprint, Winona Lake, Ind.: Eisenbrauns, 1992. Original
edition: Oxford: Oxford University Press, 1972.

Deuteronomy was composed by wisdom scribes who began
their work prior to the reforms of Josiah and continued to work
through the exilic period. [For a response, see an English translation of C. Brekelmans's 1978 article, "Wisdom Influence in
Deuteronomy," in *A Song of Power and the Power of Song: Essays on the Book of Deuteronomy,* ed. D. L. Christensen
(Winona Lake, Ind.: Eisenbrauns, 1993), 123–34. See also the
critique of J. Milgrom, *IEJ* 23 (1973): 156–61, and Weinfeld's response in the same volume, pp. 230–33.]

621 J. Milgrom. "Profane Slaughter and a Formulaic Key to the Composition of Deuteronomy." *HUCA* 47 (1976): 1–17.

Deuteronomy's law of profane slaughter (Deut. 12:15, 21), as well as its other laws, reflect a citation formula that points to an older legal source that it viewed as authoritative, namely, BC. Hence, D did not envision its laws as innovations but as implications of BC's legal theory. However, in the numerous instances in which D reflects knowledge of P's regulations, it is clear that D is a polemic against them. But it is not clear whether the P known by D was a written or oral source.

622 P. Dion. "Quelques aspects de l'interaction entre religion et politique dans le Deutéronome." *Science et Esprit* 30 (1978): 39–55.

Deuteronomy was composed as a polemic against Assyrian overlords who perpetuated their oppression via international treaties. This was accomplished by casting the text in treaty form, by presenting Yahweh as Israel's sovereign, and by adding treaty stipulations that reflected authentic Israelite legal and religious traditions.

623 P. Dion. "Deuteronomy and the Gentile World: A Study in Biblical Theology." *Toronto Journal of Theology* 1 (1985): 200–221.

Although Deuteronomy prescribes the annihilation of the Canaanites, these Canaanites did not exist at the time of the book's seventh-century B.C.E. composition. The true target of the anti-Canaanite polemic was religious syncretism. This explains why Deuteronomy can nonetheless reflect a supportive viewpoint with respect to foreigners.

624 L. Hoppe. "Deuteronomy and the Poor." *The Bible Today* 24 (1986): 371–75.

Deuteronomy views poverty as a consequence of lawless living. It addresses the problem by legislating actions, and by prescribing proper motives, for living as a healthy community of Israelites and sojourners.

625 S. D. McBride, Jr. "Polity of the Covenant People." *Int* 41 (1987): 229–44.

Deuteronomy is a social charter that reflects literary coherence and political sophistication. In this respect it serves as an archetype for modern Western constitutionalism.

626 J. H. Walton. "Deuteronomy: An Exposition of the Spirit of the Law." *Grace Theological Journal* 8 (1987): 213–25.

Deuteronomy is an extended exposition and elucidation of the Decalogue (Ten Commandments).

627   L. J. Hoppe. "Deuteronomy and Political Power." *The Bible Today* 26 (1988): 261–66.

Deuteronomy envisioned a society in which the king, like all Israelites, was under the authority of divine law. For this reason, the usual prerogatives and benefits of Near Eastern kingship—army, harem, and wealth—were forbidden to the king. The king's legal role was to read and study the law.

628   A. D. H. Mayes. "On Describing the Purpose of Deuteronomy." *JSOT* 58 (1993): 13–33.

Deuteronomy was composed during the late Judean monarchy in order to provide a new worldview in the face of Assyrian domination, which had produced an attractive alternative to traditional Yahwism.

629   G. Braulik. *The Theology of Deuteronomy.* BIBAL Collected Essays 2. North Richland Hills, Tex.: BIBAL Press, 1994.

An English translation of various essays published by Braulik in German between 1977 and 1993.

630   N. Lohfink. *The Laws of Deuteronomy: A Utopian Project for a World without Any Poor?* Cambridge: St. Edmond's College, 1996.

Published version of the 1995 Lattey Lecture (of the Von Hügel Institute). Deuteronomy's reforms sought to protect vulnerable social groups that did not have access to property for agriculture. This reform was truly a "utopian" project because it sought to eliminate the poor from ancient society.

631   T. C. Römer. "Transformation in Deuteronomistic and Biblical Historiography: On 'Book-Finding' and Other Literary Strategies." *ZAW* 109 (1997): 1–11.

Among other things, argues that the "discovery" of Deuteronomy in 2 Kings 22–23 is a common topos for legitimizing new compositions by presenting them as old. Provides numerous comparative examples from the ancient Near East.

632   M. Vervenne and J. Lust, eds. *Deuteronomy and Deuteronomic Literature: Festschrift C. H. W. Brekelmans.* BETL 133. Louvain: Peeters, 1997.

An important collection of recent perspectives on Deuteronomy, as well as on the closely related material in the Deuteronomistic History. Two of the articles are mentioned in this volume (cf. #57; #60).

633   G. Braulik. "Deuteronomy and Human Rights." *Skrif en Kerk* 19 (1998): 207–29.

The ideals reflected in the Deuteronomic law are similar in certain respects to those in the 1948 Universal Declaration of Human Rights.

634 G. Braulik. " 'Conservative Reform.' Deuteronomy from the Perspective of the Sociology of Knowledge." *OTE* 12 (1999): 13–32

Deuteronomy was the foundational document for two different Israelite movements: (1) Josiah's seventh-century B.C.E. cultic and political reforms; and (2) the sociological movement that sought return from the Babylonian exile.

635 P. D. Miller. "Deuteronomy and Psalms: Evoking a Biblical Conversation." *JBL* 118 (1999): 3–18.

The various thematic and ideological links between the Psalms and Deuteronomy suggest that the former was assembled as an expression of obedience to the latter.

636 J. G. Millar. *Now Choose Life: Theology and Ethics in Deuteronomy*. New Studies in Biblical Theology. Grand Rapids: Eerdmans, 1999.

Deuteronomy teaches that Israel should respond to divine grace in a covenant relationship. The laws of Deut. 12–26 provide the shape of this response, but Deuteronomy ultimately indicates that Israel will not keep the covenant. Millar's volume includes a survey of the study of OT ethics.

9.2 Composition, Authorship, and Context

These entries supplement those found above in chapter 3. Because the dating of Deuteronomy is often associated with the discovery of the law book in 2 Kings, it is also helpful to see the English translation of N. Lohfink's 1985 article, "Recent Discussions on 2 Kings 22–23: The State of the Question," in *A Song of Power and the Power of Song: Essays on the Book of Deuteronomy*, ed. D. L. Christensen (Winona Lake, Ind.: Eisenbrauns, 1993), 36–61.

637 G. Minette de Tillese. "Sections 'tu' et sections 'vou' das le Deutéronome." *VT* 12 (1962): 29–88.

Variations in Moses' speeches from second-person plural to second-person singular can be used to distinguish earlier elements in Deuteronomy from later elements. The earlier elements use the second-person singular (and belong to the older Deuteronomic level) while later elements use the plural forms and should be associated with the Deuteronomistic editing of Deuteronomy (e.g., chaps. 1–3). [For a historical retrospective on this issue, see C. Begg, "The Significance of the *Numerus-*

wechsel in Deuteronomy: The 'Pre-history' of the Question,"
Ephemerides theologicae lovanienses 55 (1979): 116–24.]

638 H. Cazelles. "Passages in the Singular within Discourses in the Plural of Dt 1–4." *CBQ* 29 (1967): 207–19.

Variations between singular and plural forms in Deut. 1–4 can be used to identify the original introduction to Deuteronomy, written in singular address.

639 J. Lundbom. "The Lawbook of the Josianic Reform." *CBQ* 38 (1976): 293–302.

Deut. 1–28 was composed in connection with Hezekiah's eighth-century reforms. The "lawbook" found in the days of Josiah was the appendix of Deuteronomy, Deut. 29–34 (esp. the Song of Moses in Deut. 32).

640 E. Nielsen. "Historical Perspectives and Geographical Horizons: On the Question of North-Israelite Elements in Deuteronomy." *Annual of the Swedish Theological Institute* 11 (1977–78): 77–89.

While Deuteronomy reflects northern influences because its theological movement was born there, the text itself reflects the geographical horizons of a Judean context.

641 B. Halpern. "The Centralization Formula in Deuteronomy." *VT* 31 (1981): 20–38.

Contrary to the usual view, Deuteronomy's centralization program supported existing tradition and was not an attempt to promote radical reforms.

642 R. J. Clifford. *Deuteronomy, with an Excursus on Covenant and Law.* Wilmington, Del.: Michael Glazier, 1982.

Posits the following three-stage process of growth for Deuteronomy: (1) a Josianic Deuteronomistic History (Deut. 1–3; 31:1–18; + Joshua–2 Kings); (2) the exilic insertion of the law code and framework found in Deut. 4–30; 32; and (3) P's postexilic addition of Deut. 34 and incorporation of Deuteronomy into the Pentateuch.

643 L. J. Hoppe. "Elders and Deuteronomy: A Proposal." *Eglise Théologie* 14 (1983): 259–72.

Levites, prophets, and wisdom scribes have all been suggested as the possible authors of Deuteronomy. However, the theory that Israelite elders composed the book provides the most sensible explanation for its contents.

644 G. J. Wenham. "The Date of Deuteronomy: Linch-Pin of Old Testament Criticism." *Themelios* 10, no. 3 (1985): 15–20; "The Date of Deuteronomy: Linch-Pin of Old Testament Criticism, Part 2." *Themelios* 11, no. 1 (1985): 15–18.

Examines six key categories of evidence that scholars normally use to support the view that Deuteronomy was composed at the time of Josiah's seventh-century B.C.E. reforms. Concludes to the contrary that Moses composed the Book of Deuteronomy during the second millennium B.C.E.

645 T. Römer. *Israels Väter: Untersuchungen zur Väterthematik im Deuteronomium und in der deuteronomistischen Tradition.* OBO 99. Göttingen: Vandenhoeck & Ruprecht, 1990.

In Deuteronomy, the phrase "your fathers, *Abraham, Isaac, and Jacob*" originated as "your fathers" and referred only to the exodus generation. Later editors added "Abraham, Isaac, and Jacob" in order to identity them as the forefathers. [For a critical response, see N. Lohfink, *Die Väter Israels in Deuteronomium, mit einer Stellungsnahme von Thomas Römer,* OBO 111 (Freiburg: Universitätsverlag, 1991).]

646 J. Niehaus. "The Central Sanctuary: Where and When?" *TynBul* 43 (1992): 3–30.

Scholars usually interpret "the place that Yahweh will choose" (Deut. 12:5) as a reference to Josiah's seventh-century effort to centralize worship in Jerusalem. However, this reference is intentionally ambiguous and can easily be attributed to Moses in the second millennium B.C.E.

647 E. Reuter. *Kultzentralisation: Entstehung und Theologie von Dtn 12.* BBB 87. Frankfurt am Main: Hain, 1993.

Josiah's seventh-century cult-centralizing reform was spawned by Exod. 20:22–23:33 rather than by Deuteronomy.

648 J. G. McConville and J. G. Millar. *Time and Place in Deuteronomy.* JSOTSup 179. Sheffield: Sheffield Academic Press, 1994.

Deuteronomy's altar laws do not reflect an effort to establish and centralize a permanent dwelling for the deity, and, therefore, the book's origins cannot be confidently associated with Josiah's seventh-century B.C.E. effort to centralize the cult in the Jerusalem temple. The altar laws were instead concerned with Israel's covenant faithfulness to Yahweh.

649 B. Gosse. "Deutéronome 17,18–19 et la restauration de la royauté au retour de l'exil." *Biblia e Oriente* 36 (1994): 129–38.

The "law of the king" in Deut. 17 was composed after the exile in an effort to reestablish kingship in connection with priestly institutions (as in Haggai and Zechariah).

650 J. R. Lundbom. "The Inclusio and Other Framing Devices in Deuteronomy I–XXVIII." *VT* 46 (1996): 292–315.

Literary and thematic features in Deuteronomy suggest that it is a combination of various independent collections and discourses composed during the eighth century, probably in the northern kingdom. These sources were combined in the composition of Deut. 1–28 during the seventh century.

9.3 Historical Prologue: Interpreting Deuteronomy 1–4

It was M. Noth who made popular the view that Deut. 1–3(4) did not originate as the introduction to Deuteronomy but rather as the introduction to the Deuteronomistic History in Deuteronomy–2 Kings. Other scholars have argued to the contrary that Deut. 1–3(4) is integral to the structure of Deuteronomy. Regardless of one's conclusion on the matter, it is clear that this pericope seeks to draw didactic lessons from Israel's history. For Noth's perspective, see his discussion in *The Deuteronomistic History*, 2d ed., JSOTSup 15 (Sheffield: JSOT, 1981).

651 W. A. Sumner. "Israel's Encounters with Edom, Moab, Ammon, Sihon, and Og according to the Deuteronomist." *VT* 18 (1968): 216–28.

A detailed study of Israel's encounters with Sihon, Og, Edom, Moab, and Ammon in Deuteronomy, including a comparison with the parallels in Numbers.

652 A. D. H. Mayes. "Deuteronomy 4 and the Literary Criticism of Deuteronomy." *JBL* 100 (1981): 23–51.

Deut. 4 has been inserted in its present position as part of a broader exilic redaction that cast the law book into the form of a treaty. This composition had the dual role of explaining the exile (as a curse caused by breaking the covenant) and providing hope for the future.

653 T. Veijola. "Principal Observations on the Basic Story in Deuteronomy 1–3." Pp. 249–59 in *"Wunschet Jerusalem Frieden": IOSOT Congress, Jerusalem 1986*. Edited by M. Augustin and K.-D. Schunck. BEATAJ 13. Frankfurt am Main: Peter Lang, 1988.

Attempts to unravel the "complicated literary-historical process" behind the present text in Deut. 1–3.

654 J. M. Miller. "The Israelite Journey through (around) Moab and Moabite Toponomy." *JBL* 108 (1989): 577–95.

The confusion about Israel's route through or around Moab in Numbers, Deuteronomy, and Judges reveals that the writers were not very familiar with the topography of regions south of the Arnon.

655 A. R. Millard. "King Og's Iron Bed: Fact or Fancy?" *BRev* 6, no. 2 (1990): 16–21, 44.

Og's iron bed (Deut. 3:11) was composed of a "precious metal" in the Late Bronze Age. While this was unusual, it was not entirely out of place in this early context.

656 K. Holter. "Literary Critical Studies of Deut 4: Some Criteriological Remarks." *BN* 81 (1996): 91–103.

Three major approaches to the composition of Deut. 4 (atomistic, holistic, block approaches) correspond to three different methods of analyzing the text, including changes from singular to plural (*Numeruswechsel*), changes in terminology, and changes in theme.

9.4 Parenetic Prologue: Interpreting Deuteronomy 5–11

Unlike Deut. 1–4, chapters 5–11 provide admonitions and warnings that directly inspire adherence to the law (i.e., parenesis). For this reason, many scholars believe that chapters 5–11 constitute the original prologue for Deuteronomy's laws. This pericope is introduced in chapter 5 with the Decalogue, which is the focus of §6.2.6.

657 N. Lohfink. *Das Hauptgebot: Eine Untersuchung literarischer Einleitungsfragen zu Dtn 5–11.* AnBib 20. Rome: Pontifical Biblical Institute, 1963.

The earliest version of Deut. 5–11 indicates that Deuteronomy originated as an ancient Israelite covenant at Gilgal. These materials are visible in 5:1–6:25; 9:9–19, 21, 25–29; 10:1–5, 10–18, 20–22; 11:1–17.

658 T. E. Fretheim. "The Ark in Deuteronomy." *CBQ* 30 (1968): 1–14.

Deuteronomy deemphasized the ark in its attempt to challenge monarchic authority (because the ark was a symbol of monarchic election) and emphasized the Passover as an alternative to Tabernacles (because the latter had become a corrupted festival in which the ark played a key role).

659 B. Peckham. "The Composition of Deuteronomy 5–11." Pp. 217–40 in *The Word of the Lord Shall Go Forth: Essays in Honor of David Noel Freedman in Celebration of His Sixtieth Birthday.* Edited by C. L. Meyers and M. O'Connor. Winona Lake, Ind.: Eisenbrauns, 1983.

A detailed study of Deut. 5–11 reveals that the basic "history of the covenant" in Deuteronomy–2 Kings is a single composition

(Deut. 1). This history subsequently underwent a theological redaction in Deut. 2.

660 R. C. Van Leeuwen. "On the Structure and Sense of Deuteronomy 8." *Proceedings: Eastern Great Lakes and Midwest Biblical Societies* 4 (1984): 237–49.

A refined analysis of the literary structure of Deut. 8 that pays close attention to the important role of the Deuteronomic clichés in it. Ancient Near Eastern parallels to the biblical phrase *môṣā' pî yhwh* ("what comes out of the mouth of Yahweh") are adduced. These parallels suggest that the divine word of Deut. 8 is multivalent and all-encompassing, in contrast to modern tendencies to impose an opposition of "spiritual" versus "material" upon the text.

661 V. Hurowitz. "From Storm God to Abstract Being: How the Deity Became More Distant from Exodus to Deuteronomy." *BRev* 14, no. 5 (1998): 40–47.

Biblical accounts of the Sinai theophany portray the deity differently. In Exod. 19–24, God appears on the mountain as a thundering storm, while in Deuteronomy he remains in heaven but draws up fire from the mountain toward him. In Exodus, God speaks to the people in the thunder, but in Deuteronomy God speaks with words.

9.5 The Deuteronomic Law: Interpreting Deuteronomy 12–26

As noted above, the Deuteronomic law code is usually identified with the reforms of Josiah in seventh-century Judah. Scholars commonly trace at least some of this legal tradition to an earlier period in the northern kingdom. For additional background, see §§6.2, 10.1, and 10.2.

662 Z. Zevit. "The *'EGLÂ* Ritual of Deuteronomy 21:1–9." *JBL* 95 (1976): 377–90.

The heifer ritual in Deut. 21 reflects pre-Israelite, early-Israelite, and late-Israelite phases of development.

663 R. Westbrook. "The Law of the Biblical Levirate." *RIDA* 25 (1977): 65–87.

A close reading of the Levirate law in Deut. 25 and an analysis of its legal significance in light of other biblical texts.

664 E. Bellefontaine. "Deuteronomy 21:18–21: Reviewing the Case of the Rebellious Son." *JSOT* 13 (1979): 13–31.

The capital punishment prescribed for the "stubborn and rebellious son" in Deut. 21 has in mind the obstinate people of Israel.

665 S. A. Kaufman. "The Structure of the Deuteronomic Law." *Maarav* 1 (1979): 105–58.

The coherent structure of Deut. 12–26 suggests that it is a single composition and argues against complex models of the law code's origins.

666 G. J. Wenham. "The Restoration of Marriage Reconsidered." *Journal of Jewish Studies* 30 (1979): 36–40.

Why does Deut. 24:1–4 prohibit a divorced woman from remarrying her former husband? When a woman married, she became a sister to her brother and his family. Once divorced, she was prohibited from remarrying her "brother" because of the incest laws in Lev. 18 and 20.

667 G. J. Wenham and J. G. McConville. "Drafting Techniques in Some Deuteronomic Laws." *VT* 30 (1980): 248–52.

Legal drafting techniques suggest that Deut. 22 is a single legal composition.

668 J. G. McConville. *Law and Theology in Deuteronomy.* JSOTSup 33. Sheffield: JSOT Press, 1985.

Deuteronomy is commonly associated with Josiah's seventh-century reforms and with efforts to centralize the cult in Jerusalem. However, when the laws of Deuteronomy are examined in light of the book's theology, there is nothing to prevent it from dating to the early monarchy, or even earlier. Deuteronomy's laws serve theological rather than legal functions. [For a critical response, see B. M. Levinson, "McConville's *Law and Theology in Deuteronomy*," *JQR* 80 (1990): 396–404.]

669 A. Rofé. "The Laws of Warfare in the Book of Deuteronomy: Their Origins, Intent, and Positivity." *JSOT* 32 (1985): 23–44.

Deuteronomy's laws of war do not reflect the pre- or early monarchic periods but reflect instead four viewpoints from the first-millennium Judean context: wisdom tradition, scribal tradition, zealot tradition (religious extremism that lacked tolerance), and priestly tradition. The last three phases were composed and then combined in connection with Josiah's attempt to raise a citizen army (seventh century B.C.E.). The effective context of the laws therefore disappeared with the death of Josiah at the end of the seventh century (609 B.C.E.).

670 R. K. Duke. "The Portion of the Levite: Another Reading of Deuteronomy 18:6–8." *JBL* 106 (1987): 193–201.

It is commonly believed that Deuteronomy reflects no distinction between priests and Levites and that such a distinction appeared later (or earlier) in the Priestly materials. However, the law in Deut. 18 sought to benefit the larger category of Levites—which included priests—and so cannot be taken as evidence that D's Levite/priest view differed from that of P's.

671 D. P. Wright. "Deuteronomy 21:1–9 as a Rite of Elimination." *CBQ* 49 (1987): 387–403.

In the event of an unsolved homicide, Deut. 21:1–9 prescribes
the sacrifice of a young cow in an uncultivated wadi. This elimination ritual reenacts the murder and sweeps the bloodguilt
away from the people and cultivated lands via the waters of the
wadi. Similar elimination rites appear in the Bible (e.g., Lev. 16)
and in Hittite texts.

672 A. Rofé. "The Arrangement of the Laws in Deuteronomy."
Ephemerides theologicae lovanienses 64 (1988): 265–87.

A series of older laws was used by the author(s) of Deuteronomy to compose their new code, which they arranged according to various associations. Rearranging the laws by topic will
give us some idea about the nature and structure of the source
code.

673 L. Stulman. "Encroachment in Deuteronomy: An Analysis
of the Social World of the D Code." *JBL* 109 (1990): 613–32.

Deuteronomy's laws seek to establish clear boundaries of identity to protect the Israelite community from "outsiders," particularly those living within Israelite society.

674 D. R. Daniels. "The Creed of Deuteronomy XXVI Revisited." Pp. 231–42 in *Studies in the Pentateuch*. Edited by
J. A. Emerton. VTSup 41. Leiden: Brill, 1990.

G. von Rad suggested that Deut. 26:5b–9 contained an ancient
creed from which the basic outline for the Pentateuch's was derived (#25). Although many scholars have concluded that this
"creed" is much later than von Rad thought, here it is argued
that the creed is pre-monarchic and could indeed have served
such a role in the Pentateuch's composition.

675 L. Stulman. "Sex and Familial Crimes in the D Code: A
Witness to Mores in Transition." *JSOT* 53 (1992): 47–64.

Deuteronomy's benevolence toward women is not a function of
its inherent egalitarianism but rather stems from its attempt to
transition from local- to state-oriented authority structures.

676 H. M. Barstad. "The Understanding of the Prophets in Deuteronomy." *SJOT* 8 (1994): 236–51.

Deuteronomy reflects a negative view of prophecy. The
prophecy laws in chapters 13 and 18 do not legitimize prophecy
but are instead concerned with the threat of prophetically in-
duced apostasy. [For a critique of Barstad, see K. Jeppesen, "Is
Deuteronomy Hostile towards Prophets?" *SJOT* 8 (1994): 252–56.]

677 J. Blenkinsopp. "Deuteronomy and the Politics of Post-
mortem Existence." *VT* 45 (1995): 1–16.

Deuteronomy's prohibitions regarding the death cult were motivated by a desire to supplant lineage-based kinship structures with a centralized state apparatus.

678 J. H. Tigay. "Some Archaeological Notes on Deuteronomy." Pp. 373–80 in *Pomegranates and Golden Bells: Studies in Biblical, Jewish, and Near Eastern Ritual, Law, and Literature in Honor of Jacob Milgrom.* Edited by D. P. Wright, D. N. Freedman, and A. Hurvitz. Winona Lake, Ind.: Eisenbrauns, 1995

Why does Deut. 24:6 prohibit creditors from taking an "upper millstone" as collateral? Archaeological evidence shows that this millstone, while smaller than the lower millstone, was composed of less-accessible basalt (from the Galilee region and Transjordan). This ruling therefore offered the poor some credit protections. Article includes a few other, similar observations.

679 D. Patrick. "The Rhetoric of Collective Responsibility in Deuteronomic Law." Pp. 421–36 in *Pomegranates and Golden Bells: Studies in Biblical, Jewish, and Near Eastern Ritual, Law, and Literature in Honor of Jacob Milgrom.* Edited by D. P. Wright, D. N. Freedman, and A. Hurvitz. Winona Lake, Ind.: Eisenbrauns, 1995.

Unlike the other biblical law codes, Deut. 12–26 was composed to address "Israel" as a collective entity. This rhetoric encouraged seventh-century Judah to embrace monotheism rather than polytheism.

680 P. A. Kruger. "The Removal of the Sandal in Deuteronomy xxv 9: A 'Rite of Passage'?" *VT* 46 (1996): 534–39.

Alerts us to an old proposal by the anthropologist A. van Gennep, who suggested that the removal of the sandal in Deut. 25:9 was a rite of passage marking the woman's new liberated status.

681 G. Knoppers. "The Deuteronomist and the Deuteronomic Law of the King: A Reexamination of a Relationship." *ZAW* 108 (1996): 329–46.

The Deuteronomic law of the king (Deut. 17:14–20) mandated that the king study the law but generally limited royal power. The Deuteronomistic presentation of Solomon in 1 Kings also required the king's adherence to the law but offered an expanded vision of the king's role in Israelite society.

682 E. Otto. "Treueid und Gesetz: Die Ursprünge des Deuteronomimums im Horizont neuassyrischen Vertragsrechts." *ZABR* 2 (1996): 1–52.

Form and terminology show that the original laws against inciting idolatry in Deut. 13 were composed in the mid–seventh century B.C.E. and were inspired by the loyalty oaths of the neo-Assyrian king, Esarhaddon. In this way Deuteronomy polemically substituted loyalty to Yahweh for loyalty to the Assyrian king. This text was later integrated into DC in the time of Josiah (ca. 622 B.C.E.) and then edited during the exilic and postexilic periods by Deuteronomists.

683 W. S. Morrow. *Scribing the Center: Organization and Redaction in Deuteronomy 14:1–17:13.* SBLMS 49. Atlanta: Scholars, 1995.

The original pericope of Deut. 14:1–17:13 is pre-Josianic and has as its central theme the "place" (*maqom*) where Yahweh is to be worshiped. Later additions to the text stem from the exilic period.

684 H. L. Bosman. "Redefined Prophecy as Deuteronomic Alternative to Divination in Deut. 18:9–22." *AcT* 16 (1996): 1–23.

Prophecy, divination, and other forms of intermediation were common in Mesopotamian, Canaanite, and Israelite society and were not carefully differentiated. Deut. 18:9–22 redefined and limited prophetic intermediation so that it cohered with scope of Torah as defined by Deuteronomy. This was done to legitimize the prophets as Judaism's religious leaders in the exilic community.

685 P. E. Wilson. "Deuteronomy XXV 11–12—One for the Books." *VT* 47 (1997): 220–35.

Deuteronomy reflects a cultural context that depends on shame rather than guilt as a deterrent for breaking the law and threatening social order.

686 D. I. Brewer. "Deuteronomy 24:1–4 and the Origin of the Jewish Divorce Certificate." *Journal of Jewish Studies* 49 (1998): 230–43.

The divorce legislation in Deut. 24:1–4 was composed to discourage divorce and to enable divorced women to remarry with greater ease by providing them with a divorce certificate. These benefits are in stark contrast to Near Eastern divorce law. Deuteronomy's law also prevented a husband from attempting to reclaim his wife after divorcing her for "indecency" in order to keep her dowry.

687 P. J. Marland. "Menswear and Womenswear: A Study of Deuteronomy 22:5." *Expository Times* 110 (1998): 73–76.

The purpose of the laws regulating cross-dressing was to preserve the distinction between male and female gender categories.

688 J. G. McConville. "King and Messiah in Deuteronomy and the Deuteronomistic History." Pp. 271–95 in *King and*

Messiah in Israel and the Ancient Near East. Edited by J. Day. JSOTSup 270. Sheffield: Sheffield Academic Press, 1998.

Deuteronomy presents a low view of kingship that is radically different from Near Eastern monarchic perspectives. This perspective is shared by the Deuteronomistic History in Joshua–2 Kings.

689 W. M. de Bruin. "Die Freistellung von Militärdienst in Deut. xx 5–7: Die Gattung der Wirkungslosigkeitssprüche als Schlüssel zum Verstehen eines alten Brauches." *VT* 49 (1999): 21–33.

Exemptions from military service in Deut. 20 reflect a concern for protecting life's natural patterns from disruption. This agenda is not a utopian Deuteronomic ideal but reflects instead common practice in the ancient Near East.

690 Y. Hoffman. "The Deuteronomistic Concept of the Herem." *ZAW* 11 (1999): 196–210.

The *herem* laws in Deut. 7:1–6, 20:15–18 do not cohere with the moral perspectives of Deuteronomy and hence are best viewed, both ideologically and literarily, as later additions. These additions should be associated with the postexilic composition of Joshua's conquest and carry the implication that the Canaanites no longer existed and, hence, that the law of *herem* no longer applied. This backhanded polemic was composed to contest xenophobic tendencies within the postexilic Ezra party.

691 A. C. Hagedorn. "Guarding the Parent's Honour—Deuteronomy 21.18–21." *JSOT* 88 (2000): 101–21.

The law of the stubborn and rebellious son was not intended to prescribe how problem children should be managed but was instead composed to encourage responsible child rearing.

9.6 Parenetic Epilogue: Interpreting Deuteronomy 27–30

If Deut. 5–11 provides the parenetic prologue for the book, then chapters 27–30 constitute its parenetic epilogue.

692 D. G. Schley, Jr. "Yahweh Will Cause You to Return to Egypt in Ships (Deuteronomy xxviii 68)." *VT* 35 (1985): 369–72.

Although the reference to "ships" in Deut. 28 is often emended because it seems out of place, the Assyrian annals refer to ships used on military campaigns. This reflects Assyrian control of the coasts and islands in the region and suggests that this portion of the parenetic epilogue was composed during the seventh century B.C.E.

693 A. Cholewinski. "Zur theologischen Deutung des Moab-bundes." *Bib* 66 (1985): 96–111.

> Deut. 28:69 (= Eng. 29:1) refers to a covenant between Yahweh and Israel at Moab, "besides the covenant which he had made with them at Horeb." In its present context, it is clear that this Moabite covenant is deemed more important than the Sinai event. This Moabite covenant was composed as an ancient typological precursor to the "new covenant" that was deemed necessary in the late-Judean prophetic tradition.

694 A. E. Hill. "The Ebal Ceremony as Hebrew Land Grant?" *JETS* 31 (1988): 399–406.

> The covenant ceremony in Deut. 27 is not a composite collection of tradition but reflects instead the pattern of Near Eastern royal land grants.

√ **695** T. A. Lenchak. *"Choose Life!": A Rhetorical-Critical Investigation of Deuteronomy 28:69–30:20.* AnBib 129. Rome: Pontificio Instituto Biblico, 1993.

> Explores how the rhetoric of Moses' third speech to Israel emotionally and rationally persuaded them to reject other deities and commit to a covenant relationship with Yahweh.

696 H. U. Steymans. "Eine assyrische Vorlage für Deuteronomium 28,20–44." Pp. 119–41 in *Bundesdokument und Gesetz: Studien zum Deuteronomium.* HBS 4. Freiburg: Herder, 1995.

> Parallels between the curses of Deut. 28 and those in Esarhaddon's vassal treaties indicate that Deuteronomy was influenced by the seventh-century Assyrian treaties. This influence was mediated through an Aramaic version of the treaties.

697 N. Na'aman. "The Law of the Altar in Deuteronomy and the Cultic Site near Shechem." Pp. 141–61 in *Rethinking the Foundations: Historiography in the Ancient World and in the Bible (Essays in Honour of John Van Seters).* Edited by S. L. McKenzie and T. Römer. BZAW 294. Berlin and New York: de Gruyter, 2000.

> Concern for the sacrality of Shechem in Deuteronomy (Deut. 11; 27) is usually interpreted as an older tradition that the pro-Jerusalem writers of Deuteronomy needed to include in their work. However, this Shechem tradition actually reflects an exilic development in which Shechem emerged as important after the Jerusalem temple was destroyed.

9.7 Historical and Poetic Epilogue: Deuteronomy 31–34

In its present form, Deut. 31–34 paves the way for a transition from the leadership of Moses to that of Joshua. The conclusion of the book includes the last words of Moses, two poetic "songs" in chapters 32–33, and a brief account of his death. For compositional issues relating to these chapters, see §§10.2 and 10.4.

698 C. J. Labuschagne. "The Tribes in the Blessing of Moses." Pp. 97–112 in *Language and Meaning: Studies in Hebrew Language and Biblical Exegesis (Papers Read at the Joint British-Dutch Old Testament Conference Held at London, 1973)*. Leiden: Brill, 1974.

Deut. 33 reflects a northern perspective and served two key aims: to celebrate God's guidance and to define the position of each tribe in the land. Concludes that Levi's blessing is a later Judean addition to the list.

699 H. Seebass. "Die Stämmeliste von Dtn. XXXIII." *VT* 27 (1977): 158–69.

Although the tribal list in Deut. 33 appears to include only eleven tribes, the name Jeshurun (33:4–5, 26) is actually the missing tribe, Simeon. The final form of the twelve-tribe list dates to the Davidic monarchy.

700 S. Hidal. "Some Reflections on Deuteronomy 32." *Annual of the Swedish Theological Institute* 11 (1977–78): 15–21.

The Song of Moses (Deut. 32) was composed in the postexilic period. Its ancient appearance is the result of archaizing by the author.

701 D. L. Christensen. "Two Stanzas of a Hymn in Deuteronomy 33." *Bib* 65 (1984): 382–89.

Deut. 33:2–5, 26–29 represents an older poem into which the blessings of vv. 6–25 have been placed. [Includes a survey of the study of Hebrew meter since 1960.]

702 G. A. F. Knight. *The Song of Moses: A Theological Quarry*. Grand Rapids: Eerdmans, 1995.

The Song of Moses in Deut. 32 is a Mosaic composition that was passed down orally until it was written down in the time of Solomon. Most of Knight's book offers a commentary and Christian interpretation of the song.

703 P. Sanders. *The Provenance of Deuteronomy 32*. OtSt 32. Leiden: Brill, 1996.

Contrary to one common view, which dates the Song of Moses (Deut. 32) to the exilic period, argues that the song is a preexilic composition, probably composed in the north during the late ninth or eighth centuries B.C.E.

704 S. Beyerle. *Der Mosesegen im Deuteronomium: Eine text-, compositions- und formgeschichtliche Studie zu Deuteronomium 33.* BZAW 250. Berlin and New York: de Gruyter, 1997.

The blessing of Moses in Deut. 33 was composed in three stages, including a northern *Grundschrift*, an exilic redaction that integrated the blessing into Deuteronomy, and a postexilic expansion whose focus was to link possession of the land with obedience to the law.

705 S. A. Negosian. "Linguistic Patterns of Deuteronomy 32." *Bib* 78 (1997): 206–24.

The linguistic features of Deut. 32 point to a composition date between the tenth and eighth centuries B.C.E.

10

Other Studies

706 Th. J. Meek. "The Translation of *Ger* in the Hexateuch and Its Bearing on the Documentary Hypothesis." *JBL* 49 (1930): 172–80.

The Hebrew term *ger* carries three distinct meanings in the Pentateuch, including "immigrant" (in JE), "resident alien" (in BC and D), and "proselyte" (in HC). This evidence tends to confirm source-critical views of the Pentateuch's composition.

707 J. Van Seters. "The Terms 'Amorite' and 'Hittite' in the Old Testament." *VT* 22 (1972): 64–81.

Uses of the ethnic terms "Amorite" and "Hittite" in the Hebrew Bible are similar to the use of these terms in eighth-century Assyrian texts that describe Syria-Palestine. Consequently, these terms are not evidence for the antiquity of the biblical traditions.

708 F. M. Cross, Jr., and D. N. Freedman. *Studies in Ancient Yahwistic Poetry.* 2d ed. Grand Rapids, Eerdmans, 1996. [Unchanged from original.] Original edition: SBLDS 21. Missoula, Mont.: Scholars, 1975.

A dated but important and detailed discussion of the poetry in the Song of Miriam (Exod. 15), the Blessing of Jacob (Gen. 49), and the Blessing of Moses (Deut. 33).

709 E. Neufeld. "Residual Magic in the Bible." *Dor Le Dor* 17 (1989): 255–59.

Although the Hebrew Bible contains elements that appear magical, such as the plagues in Egypt, the bronze serpent, and the red heifer, these features have been so altered by Hebrew tradition that only the outward form of magic remains. The Hebrews did not include incantations with these acts, and all supernatural effects were considered the work of God.

710 J. D. Levenson. "Exodus and Liberation." *HBT* 13, no. 2 (1991): 134–74.

Surveys and evaluates the use of the exodus tradition by liberation theologians.

711 R. W. L. Moberly. *The Old Testament of the Old Testament: Patriarchal Narratives and Mosaic Yahwism.* Minneapolis: Fortress, 1992.

The patriarchal stories are to the Mosaic tradition what the Old Testament is for the New Testament (i.e., an OT of the OT). Moberly explores the implications of this Christian theology.

712 N. Lohfink. *Theology of the Pentateuch: Themes of the Priestly Narrative and Deuteronomy.* Minneapolis: Augsburg Fortress, 1994.

An English translation of various essays published by Lohfink in German between 1961 and 1983.

713 T. Ishida. "The Lists of Pre-Israelite Nations." Pp. 8–36 in *History and Historical Writing in Ancient Israel.* Studies in the History and Culture of the Ancient Near East 16. Leiden: Brill, 1999.

Offers a history of the list of primeval inhabitants of Israel's land, which eventually reached this semi-canonical order: Canaanites, Hittites, Amorites, Perizzites, Hivites, and Jebusites.

714 D. M. Carr. "Untamable Text of an Untamable God: Genesis and Rethinking the Character of Scripture." *Int* 54 (2000): 347–62.

In Genesis and other biblical texts, the text is the product of several authors and redactors. As a consequence, the text is much more than any single author intended it to be. In this respect, both the text and the God of the text are "untamable." God meets the church in the process of reading the text.

Name Index